The IEA Health and Welfare Unit

Choice in Welfare Series No. 3

CITIZENSHIP AND RIGHTS IN THATCHER'S BRITAIN:
TWO VIEWS

Citizenship and Rights in Thatcher's Britain: Two Views

Raymond Plant

Norman Barry

London
IEA Health and Welfare Unit
1990

First published in June 1990
by
The IEA Health and Welfare Unit
2 Lord North St
London SW1P 3LB

© The IEA Health and Welfare Unit 1990

ISBN 0-255 36261-7

Typeset by the IEA Health and Welfare Unit
Printed in Great Britain by
Goron Pro-Print Co. Ltd
Churchill Industrial Estate, Lancing, West Sussex

Contents

Foreword

Citizenship and Rights in Thatcher's Britain is offered as a thought-provoking, scholarly contribution to the developing public debate about the nature of citizenship. In particular, the essays are intended for use in the teaching of social policy in schools, colleges, universities and polytechnics. Too often in the past, teaching materials have been one-sided celebrations of traditional approaches to the welfare state and have devoted inadequate attention to alternative views. By providing two original and contrasting accounts in the same volume, this collection offers a more balanced approach.

In recent years the welfare state has come under considerable criticism from all points of the political spectrum. Socialists have largely sought to repair the defences of the welfare state against what they perceive to be effective criticism from democratic capitalists; although they have also joined with classical liberals in criticising excessive bureaucracy and the lack of consumer choice. In defending the welfare state they have returned to the concept of citizenship, a notion which owes its modern origins to T.H. Marshall. Unlike many other writers on social policy, Marshall did not envisage the total replacement of the market by socialism. Rather, he saw the welfare state as complementing the market. Professor Raymond Plant, the first of our authors, has taken the lead in reviving Marshall's tradition of citizenship and placing it in the forefront of the new socialism.

In the second essay, Professor Norman Barry, examines modern citizenship theory from the standpoint of liberal capitalism. He warns that citizenship theory leads to excessive politicization and prefers that we exhaust market solutions, including benevolence and mutual aid, before resorting too quickly to the political process to solve our problems. The mixed-economy of social welfare is now firmly on the agenda.

Finally, may I once again thank the members of the Health and Welfare Unit's Advisory Council for their invaluable help and advice.

Dr David G. Green

Part 1

Citizenship and Rights

Raymond Plant

The Author

Raymond Plant has been Professor of Politics at the University of Southampton since 1979. He has specialised in 19th century political thought and has written books on Hegel, T.H. Green, and 19th century liberalism. He has also written extensively on the politics of the welfare state including a book with H. Lesser and P. Taylor-Gooby on *Political Philosophy and Social Welfare* (Routledge & Kegan Paul, London, 1981).

Professor Plant has played a leading role in the rethinking of Labour Party policy, and his essays on *Equality, Markets and the State* (1984) and on *Citizenship, Rights and Socialism* (1988) have been published as Fabian Tracts.

Introduction

The idea of empowerment is now at the centre of political debate. The neo-liberal stand, powerfully defended by the IEA in good and bad times, takes it as central that individual empowerment is best pursued through the market mechanism and that in the field of public services market provision should be extended as far as possible. In this paper I want to argue for a different case. While accepting that there is an indispensable role for the market in modern society, I shall argue that there are very clear limits to which the market can in fact empower individuals and that in the field of welfare including health and education, and public service provision generally, there is a case for considering a more complex model of empowerment, based upon the idea of citizenship rights as a complementary form of individual empowerment to that of the market. This idea is coming to have some definite political salience. Among recent examples are Paddy Ashdown's book *Citizens' Britain*[1] and Giles Radice's *Labour's Path to Power*,[2] both of which embody a citizenship approach, based upon the idea of rights. However, these books do not fully articulate the theoretical basis of the approach which they adopt and in this paper, I hope to show why such an approach to empowerment is needed as a complement to the free market. In doing this I shall seek to substantiate four claims:

(a) That the idea of citizenship and its attendant rights is now crucial for left wing politics in Britain, particularly in the welfare field, as opposed to the politics of class and interest groups.

(b) That the idea of rights is crucial in the field of welfare, where it seems to me there are compelling arguments for not extending the market at least against the existing background of inequality.

[1] Paddy Ashdown, *Citizens' Britain: A Radical Agenda for the 1990s*, London: Fourth Estate, 1989.
[2] Giles Radice, *Labour's Path to Power*, London: Macmillan, 1989.

(c) That the claim made by liberal thinkers that there is a categorical distinction to be drawn between genuine rights, which they take to be civil and political liberties, and social and economic rights, which they take to be an illegitimate extension of the idea of rights, is mistaken.

(d) That on the Left, ideas about social and economic rights, inherited from T.H. Marshall,[1] are in urgent need of rethinking if they are to be more than rhetorical.

I also hope to show that these issues are closely tied together.

Citizenship and the Left

A Politics of Common Identity

One of the great strengths of the Conservative Government in Britain since it came to power in 1979, has been its ability to appeal to what might be called a politics of common identity. That is to say, it has sought to appeal to ideas, particularly those associated with individualism, choice and the consumer which have been thought to transcend both class and interest groups in the scope of their appeal. It is assumed that behind class interests or the sectional interests of pressure groups there are a set of interests which we share in common, those to do with individual empowerment, choice and individual advancement. This has led to an emphasis on extending the role of the market which has been thought to be the paradigmatic institution for extending these values, particularly in areas previously publicly owned where it was thought producer interests and professional culture had become far too powerful in shaping the nature and delivery of services and goods. Where it has proved impossible for political reasons to privatise public services these are to be made more susceptible to market pressures or quasi-market pressures. Good recent

---

[1] Marshall, T.H., *Citizenship and Social Class*, Cambridge: Cambridge University Press, 1950.

examples of these are the proposed reforms in the National Health Service, the proposals for the reform of the legal profession, the impact of the Education Reform Act on schools, and the White Paper on extending the role of fees in the financing of universities. All of these changes, while stopping well short of pure market solutions, nevertheless involve an extension of the market, as in the internal market proposals for the NHS and the role of fees in universities, or they involve surrogate market solutions as in the reforms in schools. In all of these cases the effect, so it is argued, will be to empower the individual consumer of the service against the producer groups and to increase the range of methods of exit from a particular form of a publicly provided service.

There are two aspects of this strategy which I shall focus upon. They relate to the first two themes about citizenship, the politics of the Left and the role of the market and citizenship.

The first aspect on which I will concentrate is the issue of the individual consumer as a bearer of common identity within an otherwise pluralistic society. Either the Left responds to this in a similar way, in its attempt to build up an alternative idea of a common identity, or it develops the other two strategies available to it which are a class-based approach or one based upon interest groups. I shall argue, throughout the paper, in terms of an approach based upon citizenship as a basis for the politics of the Left because the two alternatives seem to me to be hopeless strategies for the Left to follow in the 1990s.

Problems of a Class-Based Strategy

If the Left adopts a class-based strategy, seeing itself as the political instrument for defending class interests, then there are two fatal problems, which are too well known for me to need to spend much time on them. The first is that the Left assumes that there is a common class interest to be found in the working class, but this seems to be false in terms either of survey evidence, or in terms of voting patterns in the 1980s. Unless one brings into play some epistemologically rather dubious notion of false consciousness, it is very difficult to argue on any evidential basis that working-class people actually share one common political or economic interest.

Second, the class nature of politics is now too restricted for a reasonable electoral appeal to be made on that basis. There has been a decline in the manual working class and even if they do share a common political interest, this is going to be too narrow a basis for a politics of the Left. This does not mean that the working class is unimportant to the Left, but there has to be a way of reaching out beyond working-class interests while at the same time formulating policies which will incorporate such interests. I shall argue that the citizenship approach does this.

An Interest-Group Strategy

The alternative is to argue in favour of a strategy based upon interest groups; to see the Left as a coalition of such groups. However, this approach also has severe difficulties and in my view puts the political cart before the horse. If a political stance is to be defined in terms of aggregating the interests of particular groups then there are two obvious problems. The first is that not all the interests will be compatible and there is the need for some political stance beyond interest groups which will allow decisions to be made between incompatible aims. Alternatively, the Left will merely go for the lowest common denominator among interest groups which it recognises. In the first case there is a need for a framework of values against which the claims of rival interest groups can be assessed. In the second, there will be the rather unheroic approach which defines a political programme in terms of a minimum framework of agreement. Far from seeing politics as the aggregation of interest groups, there is a need for a basic ideological stance which will set criteria of recognition of interest group claims and their arbitration when they conflict with one another.

The Alternative — Citizenship

There is therefore a need to reach out beyond class interest because this is not homogeneous and is too small a base for a politics of the Left, and there is also a need to go beyond the fragmentary politics of interest groups. The idea of citizenship can provide a framework for going beyond both the limits of class and the fragmentation of interests. Citizenship offers the basis for a new approach to some idea of common identity and an alternative to the present government's appeal to individualism and consumer choice as the basis for such an identity. Today, in my view, such an account of citizenship has to be in terms of rights and obligations in order to provide such a framework to politics. So, having made my claim about the salience of the idea of citizenship to the Left, I can now move on to my second claim, that citizenship and its attendant rights and obligations provides a real alternative to the market-based approach, in terms of individualism and consumer sovereignty.

Markets and Liberty

In the past four or five years Labour politicians have been arguing that the aim of socialism is the extension of freedom, coupled with the argument that the market, while important, is not sufficient for this purpose. This has been a theme of Roy Hattersley's *Choose Freedom*,[1] and Bryan Gould's *Socialism and Freedom*,[2] together with Giles Radice's book on revisionism.[3] It is also a central theme of Labour's policy

---

[1] Roy Hattersley, *Choose Freedom: The Future for Democratic Socialism*, London: Michael Joseph, 1987.

[2] Bryan Gould, *Socialism and Freedom*, London: Macmillan, 1985.

[3] Radice, *op. cit.*

8

review document, *Social Justice and Economic Efficiency*. In this section, I shall explore the philosophical issue at stake in the claim that the market is not the most effective means for extending freedom, and argue that central to a new form of social democracy is the establishment of a set of citizenship rights to social and economic resources outside the market. What is at issue here is whether empowerment and individual freedom are to be found in the market and the role of the consumer within it, or in a more complex and messy conception of citizenship. This conception sees a central role for markets but for good reasons views citizenship as the basis of common identity rather than the individual as a consumer.

The Left's Critique of the Neo-Liberal Market

It seems to me that the Left sees three central defects in the neo-liberal idea of extending the role of the market as much as possible in society. These defects are that the neo-liberal operates with a defective view of liberty, a defective critique of social justice, and an over-reliance on the trickle-down effect as the means of empowerment. However, before looking at the Left's critique of these ideas, I should say what I believe is central to the neo-liberal argument.

Freedom

The argument about freedom appears essentially twofold, partly to do with the analysis of liberty and partly to do with the neo-liberal account of markets. The view of liberty is that it is essentially negative, that is to say it is the absence of intentional coercion. Therefore, I am unfree when an identifiable agent prevents me from doing what I would otherwise choose to do. This has two very important consequences for the argument about freedom, empowerment and markets. The first is that, as it stands, it entails a categorical distinction between freedom and ability. That is to say, the issue of whether I have the ability and the resources necessary to do something is separate from the question of whether I am free to do it. Neo-liberals have seen the issue at stake here between Left and Right in that if ability and freedom are logically linked, then in order to extend freedom to all, it would be necessary to produce a redistribution of resources in order to extend the abilities of those who lack the resources to do what they would choose to do. However, the claim that there is a logical distinction between freedom and ability blocks this argument.

The reasons for distinguishing freedom from ability are twofold. First, it is argued that if freedom is defined as the ability to fulfil my desires then this is a claim that I am unfree unless I am omnipotent, which is absurd. Equally, the freedom of the poor person with wide-ranging desires will be different from the degree of freedom of a similar person with more restricted tastes. It is absurd to link liberty differentially to individual desire. This leads to the second reason for wanting to distinguish freedom from ability. If we accept the liberal idea of equal freedom, then it cannot be achieved if we link freedom and ability because if, per impossible, we could equalise ability at time $T(1)$ this distribution will have changed at $T(2)$ and inequality will reassert itself. However, if freedom is defined as the absence of intentional coercion, then it is possible through a framework of abstract laws to secure such a form of freedom. This argument has a direct impact on the case for freedom and the market in two respects. First, the outcomes of market transactions, which leave some richer than others, do not affect the issue of liberty if it is logically distinct from ability and associated resources. In terms of the absence of coercion under abstract rules, the poor man is as free as the rich man. Secondly, as I have already said, there is no argument in terms of liberty, and resources are different things. The political rub here is, as Sir Keith Joseph argued in *Equality*,[1] 'Poverty is not unfreedom'.

[1] Joseph, K., and Sumption, J., *Equality*, London: John Murray, 1979. The whole of the argument in these paragraphs is drawn from F.A. Hayek's *The Constitution of Liberty*, London: Routledge & Kegan Paul, 1960.

The second central argument about freedom and the market links this understanding of liberty to a characterisation of markets — that the outcomes of markets are unintended and unforeseeable for individuals — which seems to me to be central to the neo-liberal position. Given this claim, then outcomes cannot infringe freedom because they are unintended and freedom can only be limited by intentional coercion.

Taking these arguments together, it then follows that there is no case in terms of freedom for securing a social and economic status of citizenship outside the market. Citizenship is confined to a narrow field, being defined in terms of obedience to the abstract laws which prohibit mutual coercion and not in terms of rights and entitlements to economic and social resources. The market or economic sphere generally must be depoliticised as far as possible. Within the market what matters is the consumer and his or her choices. So long as market exchanges are uncoerced at the individual level the market cannot infringe freedom.

The other legitimate role for citizenship is active citizenship defined in essentially non-political terms as acting in voluntary groups and agencies, particularly in charitable and welfare related fields.

Social Justice and the Market

This argument is replicated in the neo-liberal attack on the idea of social justice. The neo-liberal sees social justice as essential to the socialist case whether in its marxist or revisionist form. However, it is regarded as a fatally flawed notion and as embodying no cogent moral demands in terms of which the market should be constrained. There are several strands to this argument which I will refer to without much elaboration.

The first argument essentially uses the same kind of characterisation of markets as producing unintended and unforeseeable outcomes as a ground for saying that in a general way the market cannot produce injustice. Like coercion, injustice has to be the result of an intentional act. However, given the understanding of markets offered by the neo-liberal, market outcomes are not unjust whatever they may yield; there can only be distributive injustice where there is a distributor. However, since the outcomes of markets are the unintended outcomes of a myriad acts of exchange there is in fact no distribution of income and wealth and, therefore, there can be no maldistribution, so long as individual acts of exchange are not coerced.

In addition, it is argued that in a morally pluralist society we have no way of coming to some objective agreement about the various contending criteria of social justice. These may be, for example, distribution according to need, desert, merit, or entitlement; utilising these different criteria will yield different distributions of resources. However, in the view of the neo-liberal, given moral pluralism, we have no way of reaching agreement on the priority of different criteria. Even if we could, we would soon disagree about the meaning of the different criteria. On this view there is no consensual account of what needs are, or of what merit and desert consist. These will differ according to different moral frameworks. Because of this a regime which seeks to achieve social justice will act in an arbitrary and discretionary way because public officials charged with meeting needs or recognising merit have no agreed standards which could be elaborated as rules to guide their distributive tasks. In turn, as a result of this inherent vagueness and ambiguity at the heart of a public policy which seeks social justice, baneful political effects will follow. Because there are no agreed values of social justice, interest groups animated by their own assumptions of what social justice requires will look to government to satisfy their own inherently disputable demands. This means that the most powerful groups are likely to obtain concessions from government to meet what they see as social justice, while less powerful groups are likely to resent the government for failing to meet their own equally disputable claims. In a situation in which we lack what Hegel called '*Sittlichkeit*' — an agreed morality — social justice, far from constraining the market, becomes a camouflage for special pleading by interest groups, with the likely effects being as I have suggested.

Trickle Down and the Free Market

A concern with social justice may be a perfectly understandable but misguided result of a concern about poverty in society. Because according to the neo-liberal view poverty, correctly understood, is going to be cured more effectively by the trickle-down effect of a free market rather than through state action to secure a social and economic status outside the market. I say 'correctly understood', because it would appear that neo-liberals by and large reject what has come to be called the relative view of poverty, where poverty is seen in terms of a failure to attain a standard of consumption which is regarded as some kind of norm relating to a standard of citizenship in society. This view animates Peter Townsend's book on *Poverty in the United Kingdom*.[1] However, it is rejected by neo-liberals partly because they do not see how the idea of relative poverty can be disentangled from the idea of inequality. To solve the problem of relative poverty would require a more egalitarian society which assumes that we have consensual criteria of equality which we do not possess, which would imply a large-scale distributive state, and which will have an adverse effect on economic dynamism given the view about the need for incentives which such dynamism requires.

Poverty is better understood as a kind of absolute standard in the sense that what matters is not what the gap is between the rich and the poor, but whether the poor are better or worse off on their own terms as time passes. In the neo-liberal view poverty in this sense will be met best by the free

---

[1] London: Penguin Books, 1979.

market's trickle-down effect, so that what the richer sections of society consume today will, over time, trickle-down to the poorer sections of society.

So there is no case, as far as the neo-liberal is concerned, for moral constraints on the market in terms of freedom and social justice, no need for the state to secure a specified standard of living and a status independent of the market, and no case for defining citizenship in terms of social and economic rights. What matters is that citizenship is seen in narrow terms of the state securing mutual non-coercion with empowerment of individuals coming as the result of the trickle-down effect of the market. The only other aspects of citizenship are seen in terms of private voluntary action of the sort which I mentioned earlier.

A Response from the Left

While the neo-liberal arguments, set out in the previous chapter, constitute a powerful critique of the socialist view of citizenship in relation to the market, they can I think be answered in each respect. And doing so will provide the Left with the moral basis of a citizenship approach which will then need to be elaborated in institutional and policy terms: the theme of the final part of this essay.

Defects in the Liberal Approach to Freedom and Autonomy

There are a number of defects in the liberal approach to freedom and autonomy which, as I have argued, is construed as mutual non-coercion. The fundamental problems relate to the distinction drawn between freedom and ability on the one hand and the characterisation of markets on the other. If freedom and ability are separate, then we have to ask the neo-liberal what is valuable about liberty, autonomy, and empowerment, as they see it? Surely, the answer to the question of why liberty is valuable is because being free from coercion allows us to live a life shaped by our own values and ends. This, I believe, is the liberal ideal. But if that is so, then as Rawls[1] has argued, liberty is valuable differentially depending on whether one has or has not got the resources to live such a life shaped by one's own ends. Even if liberty is defined in negative terms its value will differ between individuals depending on their level of resources. Should it not, therefore, be part of the liberal aim to secure as fair a value of liberty as we can get as a society?

Freedom and Ability

This argument can be used to question the idea of negative liberty in a more fundamental way, in the sense that what makes liberty valuable is that we are enabled to do things with the space within which we are not coerced by others. However, if it is this ability which makes freedom valuable then it could be argued that there is a conceptual link between freedom and ability; it is our ability to do things which makes freedom worth struggling for. In this case, there is a logical link between freedom and ability, and a negative view of liberty is not sustainable on its own. It is this understanding which animates MacCallum's idea that freedom has to be seen as a triadic concept which includes an account of:

(a) The agents who are free.
(b) The restrictions or limitations which they are free from.
(c) What it is they are free to do or not to do.[2]

The liberal rejects this third item and emphasises the first two. However, as I have argued, this is inadequate because it is not then possible to give an account of why freedom, the central value of liberalism, is in fact valuable to us.

Therefore, there are, in my view, good reasons for dismissing the liberal rejection of the link between freedom and ability. And this rejection has crucial political consequences because

---

[1] Rawls, J., *A Theory of Justice*, Oxford: The Clarendon Press, 1973.
[2] MacCallum, R.B., 'Negative and Positive Freedom', *Philosophical Review*, Vol. 76, 1967.

the liberal view blocks any argument for redistribution of resources in terms of freedom.

Liberalism and Needs

Of course the liberal will reply that the argument may fall into the acute difficulty that we do not possess an account of those abilities which are supposed to be central to the exercise of liberty. If we argue that it is the job of the state to secure resources to match abilities, and that we value freedom to enable us to satisfy our desires, then it would follow that it is the duty of the state to secure those resources which will enable us to satisfy our desires, which is an absurd position. If on the other hand we try to define a set of core abilities or needs then we are back with the problem of moral pluralism; that in a morally diverse society we have no basis of agreement to determine which abilities are more central to our notion of freedom than others, and we have no way of settling this question. However, this assumes too much in the way of moral pluralism even for the liberal's own comfort. Take just two examples of the way in which liberals themselves actually operate with an idea of needs which is after all what we are talking about. In *The Constitution of Liberty*,[1] Hayek argues that a monopoly in an essential resource is coercive. Now one could think of various reasons why a monopoly would be undesirable, but how can a monopoly be coercive unless, first of all, there is a link between liberty and the possession of resources? And further, it implies that we have a clear view of what are essential resources, in the sense of resources which meet human needs. I claim, therefore, that, however tacitly, Hayek is arguing that there is a link between freedom and basic needs and that we must have a criterion for determining basic needs if we are to say which monopolies are coercive and which are not.

---

[1] *Op. cit.*, Chapter 9.

16

Liberalism, Poverty and Needs

The same sort of argument applies in the context of poverty. The point could be made in terms of Hayek's argument that the welfare state is concerned with an absolute level of poverty which again might be thought to imply an account of needs. The point can also be made with reference to Sir Keith Joseph's work *Stranded on the Middle Ground*[1] in which he argues that poverty is to be defined in terms of the needs of the poor rather than the expenditure of the rich. This may or may not be a good argument against the relative view of poverty, but it certainly operates with a conception of needs, if it is to have any force. Hence, it does seem to me that the liberal cannot dismiss the idea that freedom is concerned with the satisfaction of needs precisely because this idea is reflected in their own claims about the nature of poverty, and in terms of their view about the coercive nature of monopolies in some sorts of goods.

I therefore conclude that the liberal argument, that there can be no moral case for constraining the market because of their understanding of freedom, is fatally flawed in terms of assumptions which liberals themselves accept. If a poverty floor or a welfare minimum, defined in terms of needs, is the basis of the neo-liberal's absolutist conception of poverty then the neo-liberal can hardly use two arguments against needs which are usually central to their critique. The first criticism is that needs are open-ended and should not be used in arguments about social policy; the second follows from this — since needs are open-ended, they can be bid up by interest-group pressures which have the baneful effects which we saw in the context of social justice. However, they cannot have it both ways, to argue against a relative view of poverty by invoking

---

[1] 'An absolute standard of means is defined by reference to the actual needs of the poor and not by reference to the expenditure of those who are not poor. A family is poor if it cannot afford to eat.' London: Centre for Policy Studies, 1976, p. 7.

a notion of need, however tacitly, and then criticising the socialist or social democrat for using what they regard as this vague and open-ended idea as part of what they understand by social justice. Of course, the liberal might reply that this is not much of a concession on their part because the idea of the welfare state meeting basic needs falls a long way short of the way in which socialists want to use the idea of need as a principle of distributive justice, going far beyond some minimal level. However, there are two replies to this. The first is that, as I have said, if you invoke the idea of need, then you are in fact invoking an open-ended kind of idea, and there is no clear stopping place between its use in what the liberal sees in a minimalist sense and in what the socialist or social democrat sees in a more maximalist way.

Markets, Freedom and Social Justice

The second part of the argument is about the nature of markets which, I established earlier, was central to the neo-liberal account of the relation between the market and freedom, and social justice and the market. Because coercion can be caused only by intentional action, and because injustice can only occur in the same way, it follows that in terms of their outcomes markets cannot infringe liberty or cause injustice. The crux of the case is that market outcomes are unintended and unforeseeable. And it seems to me to be only sensible to accept that the outcomes of markets are unintended. However, this does not settle the question of whether markets can infringe liberty or cause injustice. Part of the issue here depends on the foreseeability of market outcomes and also on the nature of our moral approach to unintended but alterable processes.

Market Outcomes

Let us first concentrate on the issue of unforeseeability. Of course, the liberal is not arguing that market outcomes are unforeseeable in general. How could he? The cogency of his proposals to extend markets depends precisely on the fact that they are foreseeable — they will produce more efficiency, they will increase supply, they will extend consumer choice, etc. If market outcomes were in general unforeseeable these claims could not be made, let alone substantiated. The claim rather is that they are unforeseeable for individuals. However, does this make any moral difference? It has never been part of the claim of socialists that the bad consequences of markets had to be foreseeable at the individual level for injustice and coercion to occur. The claim has been in terms of groups, that those with least are likely to leave the market with least. If this is a foreseeable general result of markets, and I would argue that it is, does this make any moral difference to the status of markets? I believe that it does, in that the liberal wants to claim that the unintended and unforeseeable outcomes of markets mean that we bear no collective responsibility for their outcome. However, while markets may have these features we can still be held responsible for the unintended but foreseeable consequences of our actions. If the impact of markets on those with least resources is as I have suggested, then while these consequences may be unintended they are foreseeable. And if this is so we can be held to bear collective responsibility for the outcomes and further, it can be claimed, that markets are not in principle unprincipled. This is particularly the case when the outcomes are capable of being altered.

Certainly a natural process such as an earthquake may produce an outcome which is unintended and could not be foreseen and this is why those who suffer have not had their freedom infringed or an injustice done to them, but *pace* Hayek and his followers, markets are not like this. General outcomes can be foreseen and they are alterable and in this sense we can regard their outcomes as coercive even though they are unintended. This is particularly true if, as I have suggested, there is a logical link between freedom, needs, and resources.

Markets and Social Justice

Markets for the same reasons can produce injustice. At the level of personal morality an unintended but foreseeable consequence of my actions may be to deprive you of resources, and the foreseeability of my action makes me responsible for the outcome even if it is unintended. To act in such a way would be unjust. Similarly, at the level of the market the fact that its consequences are in general foreseeable means that there can still be a moral critique of it in terms of social justice.

Of course, the liberal will then revert to the claim that we lack any clear criteria of social justice in terms of which to constrain markets. Yet, this is not so even on the liberal's own assumptions because, as I have argued, he tacitly operates with a notion of needs; those needs which bear most clearly on the capacity for action and agency which are necessary conditions for achievement of the liberal values of freedom and autonomy. Of course, it is true that the liberal will claim elsewhere that needs are not an adequate criterion for social justice because even those needs of agency such as health, income, education, and security, are open-ended and can be pushed up by interest group pressures and hence are likely to become heavily politicised. This is all true but unless we abandon the liberal's own commitment to a basic standard of welfare based upon needs so can the needs which the liberal must invoke in order to ground his own idea of the proper scope of welfare.

Overall then, it does seem to me that the liberal has not got a cogent moral case for denying a constraint on market outcomes in terms of freedom and social justice, at least in so far as the latter is seen as a necessarily politicised account of needs. Securing the resources to meet such needs is, a central aspect of citizenship in relation to welfare and can be defined in terms of rights. However, before moving to my last two claims I have to defend this view against the final part of the neo-liberal critique. This is that even if the moral case which I have made is cogent, there is still the practical point that the free market is still better than social justice as a way of meeting these needs, and of empowering all individuals as autonomous agents — even at the cost of greater inequality.

Justice, Power and Markets

There are two aspects to my response to this, only one of which I can consider here since I have dealt with it at some length elsewhere.[1] The first aspect, and the one which I shall not discuss, is the empirical basis of the claim that the trickle-down effect, free of government redistribution, will empower the poor more than social justice. I do not think that the empirical evidence of the last ten years shows this claim to be unambiguously true. There is also a logical or conceptual issue at stake to do with the idea of the market empowering people. If power is an open-ended notion so that more and more of it can be created then, I suppose, it might be claimed, subject to the empirical evidence, that the market does empower people more and more as it increases resources. But this is to assume that power is not a relational concept. If it is, the picture gets more murky because then it could be argued that empowerment is a zero-sum game in which some people can gain more power only at the expense of others. And, if power is a positional good, then empowerment cannot trickle down.

Power as a Positional Good

Why might we think of power as a positional good? Consider the discursive account of positional goods given by Fred Hirsch in *The Social Limits to Growth*.[2] Standing on tiptoe to watch a game is a positional good in the sense that if only I

[1] Hoover, K. and Plant, R., *Conservative Capitalism in Britain and the United States: A Critical Appraisal*, London: Routledge, 1988.
[2] Fred Hirsch, *The Social Limits to Growth*, London: Routledge & Keegan Paul, 1977.

do it I gain a positional advantage over those in front of me. But the more people who do it the less valuable standing on tiptoe becomes and when everyone does it the advantage disappears altogether. So it might be argued, the same is true of power. When it is possessed equally it disappears. If we accept Dahl's[1] account of power, that A exercises power over B if he prevents B doing what he would otherwise do, then it would follow that if power were equally shared it would disappear, just as the value of standing on tiptoe disappears when all do it. Thus, it seems to me, there is a strong case for saying that power is a positional good, which means that it cannot be subject to the trickle-down effect. This means that the poor cannot be empowered just because their lot improves in absolute terms if their relative position declines, which it indisputably has after 10 years of neo-liberalism in economic policy. The poor can be empowered only if their position is improved relative to the rich and this cannot be achieved through the market.

Thus, I rest my case over my first two claims that there is a basis for claiming a central place for securing a status of citizenship in social and economic terms outside the market because the market cannot *by itself* empower the poor: it cannot secure the means of meeting the needs, including power and autonomy, which are necessary for the achievement of the freedom and autonomy which is the liberal ideal, and that there is a case for seeing the market constrained in the interests of social justice based upon an idea of the needs of agency. In the second positive part of the paper I shall argue that these needs can form the basis of a set of rights, but that the idea of welfare rights ought to be rethought.

---

[1] Dahl, R., 'The Concepts of Power', in Bell, R., Edwards, D., and Wagner, R., (eds), *Political Power: A Reader in Theory and Research*, New York: Free Press, 1969, p. 18.

A Defence of Positive Rights

It is central to the coherence of the liberal vision to deny that
there is a moral right to an economic and a social status
independent of the market. While formal civil and political
rights are of course made immune from the market as formal
rights, the liberal cannot extend this idea of rights to resources
without destroying a good deal of the positive argument in
favour of the market. I do not believe that there are cogent
arguments for restricting rights to civil and political ones. A
coherent case can be made for extending rights to include
social and economic ones, although, as I have argued, what
this actually means in practice has to be rethought.

Liberalism and Rights

The basic reason why liberals do not believe in the extension
of the idea of rights to the social and economic field is the
fact of scarcity. There can be no enforceable right to scarce
resources and without the idea of enforceability the idea of a
right becomes merely rhetorical. In this context a distinction
is frequently drawn between positive rights to resources which
welfare rights would imply and negative rights which it is
assumed civil and political rights are. In some ways this mirrors
the distinction which we met earlier between negative and
positive liberty. Negative liberty requires the absence of
coercion and civil and political rights protect liberty in this
sense because they define an area of non-coercion. Civil and
political rights essentially imply duties of forbearance. I respect
your right to freedom of expression by not interfering in what
you say; I respect your right to life by not killing you; I
respect your right to privacy by not invading it; I respect your
bodily integrity by not raping and assaulting you; and so on.
The duties which are correlative to rights are duties of
forbearance, of abstaining from action. As such they do not
run up against the limits of scarcity. As Charles Fried the

Harvard lawyer put it, 'How can we run out of people not harming each other, leaving each other alone?'[1]

Rights and Duties

Social and economic rights, however, are paradigmatically rights to resources. Thus, for example, the right to life is interpreted in a positive way as not just implying not being killed, but also as a right to the means to life. The duties which correlate with negative rights are duties which require one to forbear from action. There are duties which are essentially costless, and are what philosophers have called perfect duties in the sense that they can always be fulfilled. Positive rights, however, run up against the problem of scarcity and cannot always be fulfilled. Therefore, the duties which correlate with positive rights are imperfect and, as such, they cannot be coerced by the state for example through the tax system. This distinction, it is claimed, has a number of important theoretical and practical consequences. The first is that a right must be enforceable if there is any point in calling it a right. The reason for this is that if rights are claimed simultaneously against scarce resources then not every right holder can, in fact, secure what is claimed under the right. In these circumstances there will have to be some rule which rations the distribution of resources to the right holders, and this rule cannot itself be based upon the idea of a right but will probably have to be a utilitarian or consequentialist one. That is to say, how the resources are allocated will have to be judged not against the enforceable claims of the right holder, but against some conception of the most effective use of resources, effectiveness being judged in terms of welfare and utility. However, if rights routinely have to give way to considerations of utility, in what sense are they still rights?

[1] Charles Fried, *Right and Wrong*, Cambridge, Mass: Harvard University Press, 1978, p. 110.

Second it is argued that in the case of negative rights the correlative duty is clear and categorical. It is not to kill, not to assault, not to coerce and not to interfere: we know what the duties are and we know when we have discharged them. In the case of positive rights, however, this is not the case, because they are essentially vague and open-ended. Take the two interpretations of the right to life. On the negative view the duty not to kill is clear and categorical and does not give rise to ambiguity, whereas the positive right to life is open-ended in the sense that there is a duty on someone to secure to me all those resources which will keep me alive. In the medical case, for example, there is, from the negative view, a clear right not to be killed and we can formulate this in terms of a clear rule which can be enforced. Thus we have laws prohibiting both voluntary and involuntary euthanasia. But, if the right to life is a right to medical resources, this can never be formulated as a rule since what it implies is subject to the constraint of scarcity and is bound to involve a degree of discretionary judgement which is absent in the negative case.

Rights and Scarcity

However, it is arguable that the security of the distinction which the liberal wishes to draw between the two sorts of rights is very doubtful. The reason why it is dubious is that the issue of scarcity is much more pervasive than the liberal will typically allow. Negative rights, like positive rights, require resources once it is allowed that there is, along with the idea of a right, the idea of its enforceability which, after all, is the idea which the liberal brings into play in trying to deny the legitimacy of positive rights. That is to say, if I have a right to have a negative right implying non-coercion enforced when it is infringed, then clearly this requires the state as the guarantor of the right to commit resources to its enforcement. These resources will include the police, courts, legislation, prisons, and so forth. This is because in the real world there is, in fact, not just a scarcity in material goods, but also in motivation in relation to forbearance. Take two examples of negative rights such as a right to privacy and a right to security. The fact is that people do not always forbear. They do infringe such rights and to prevent such infringements there is the need for safeguards such as the Data Protection Act, street lighting, and checks at airports, which go as far as possible to secure such rights. These are scarce resources and the demands embodied in the rights in question run up against this constraint. Recall the argument that the duties related to negative rights, unlike positive rights, are clear and categorical. Obviously this claim does not hold in the sense that securing the implementation of these rights is going to involve costs of various sorts and these costs, for example what kinds of legislation in respect of data protection, or what level of policing, or what degree of street lighting, are going to be a matter of political negotiation just as much as the resources to meet positive rights to education, health, and welfare.

Several conclusions follow from this. The first is that the argument that positive rights involve open-ended commitments in a way that securing negative rights do not is fatally flawed. For example, in the medical case it is argued there can be no right to medical care because of the open-ended nature of medical need which grows with technological change. But the same is true of the rights to privacy and security. There was no need for the Data Protection Act before the computer; there was no need for elaborate security precautions at airports before the invention of such things as plastic explosives. The enforceability of negative rights is therefore also open-ended, just as positive rights are. However, this is not seen as an insuperable obstacle to the idea of continuing to have such rights. We are assured, for example, that there is no such thing as absolute security, but it is still thought worthwhile to state that we have a right to be able to travel securely. Why cannot the same be true for social and economic rights? Clearly there cannot be a right to some kind of absolute level of medical provision but why is this thought to be a fatal argument against the idea that there can be a right to health care?

Thus rights such as the right to privacy are genuine rights and there is no sense in the idea of some kind of absolute degree of protection of such rights. So the obvious point to make is that we can through normal political negotiation arrive at some kind of consensus about what would be, at a particular time, an adequate degree of public provision to protect such rights. If we can do this in relation, say, to the right to privacy or security, why could we not arrive at such a degree of consensus in relation, for example, to education or health care?

Rights and Resources

Let us spend a moment or two looking at the health-care example to explore the idea that, as with the right to privacy, we can arrive at a degree of consensus about what health care requires in resource terms. In order to make progress with such an idea there have to be concessions from both the Right and the Left. The Right will have to abandon the claim that health is different from the right to privacy because of scarcity and because of its open-ended nature, because, as we have seen, the situation in reality is not as simple as that. On the Left it means accepting the idea that there is a limit to what can be done and trying to find a basis of consensus against a background of scarcity.

There are two aspects which such a consensus would have to incorporate. The first is obviously over the nature of the resources to be committed to health care, the second is about their just allocation. This latter issue is vital because part of my argument is that a right to a social resource, whether in medicine or privacy, is in part to do with a right to a just allocation of those resources. At the minimum, a just allocation of resources to the individual from the resources of a society dedicated to health is going to require the equal opportunity to acquire such resources, and this is going to mean that each individual's interest in health should be treated with equal concern and respect. That is to say, there is no antecedent reason why one person's interests in health should be taken as having greater importance than anyone else's. This principle would then require any health-care system compatible with the idea of rights to involve the idea of equality of access to health resources. So, the right to health care would require as part of the consensus about both resources and the nature of their distribution a commitment to equality of access or opportunity to such resources. In this sense, therefore, the idea of having a right to health care would require this procedural notion to be in place, and the same would be true by parity of reasoning for other welfare rights such as the right to education or social security.

Degree of Resource Provision

What about a consensus on the nature or degree of resource provision? I do not think that this can be a conceptual issue any more than what privacy and security need for their protection can be a conceptual issue. These are fundamentally matters for political negotiation, but this does not invalidate the issue. It is possible to try to argue for some bench-marks in relation to the degree of resource provision, in addition to equality of access. Take two examples which are often discussed in the American literature. The first is to try to define a set of basic medical needs and related basic services as, for example, argued by Professor Alain Enthoven in his Consumer Choice Health Plan which includes physician services, inpatient and outpatient hospital services, emergency services, mental health provision, laboratory and X-ray services.[1] That is to say, we must try to define a core set of health needs and their implied resources. He goes on to argue that, at least for some groups, this entitlement might be

---

[1] Enthoven, A.C., *Health Plan: The Only Practical Solution to the Soaring Costs of Medical Care*, Reading: Addison-Wesley, 1980.

defined in terms of a voucher which he states would imply, at 1980 prices, £1,350 for a family of four on an income of £4,200. While a great deal in Enthoven's proposals is questionable, nevertheless, implicit in his argument is the idea that we can define a set of needs and provisions to which there would be an entitlement and equality of access. There is nothing in this approach which would imply that it is more difficult in principle to define a right or an entitlement in this context than in the sphere of privacy or, to take another positive right, education where, in this country at least, we have a fairly high degree of consensus about what basic educational resources should be.

Level of Resource Provision

However, the fact that Enthoven is able to put a price on what he believes an adequate level of provision, means that he is going beyond defining the set of basic health needs and is implying an idea of what the level of provision should be. This might be done in two ways, one which would be rather minimalist the other more expansive. We might for example take the average consumption of health care over a number of years and try to define an entitlement in terms of that average. We might then agree that public expenditure on health should provide the resources for equality of access to such an average level of consumption. Alternatively, we could argue in a way which might suit the Left more: that since the middle classes take a disproportionate share of NHS resources we should define the average, not across total provision, but as the average middle-class provision and define entitlements in terms of that average. While the second view would be more congenial to the Left, it still involves recognising a limit to provision. I believe that this is only realistic however, and it would be better to have this limit defined in a transparent way and linked to entitlements rather than relying on the discretion of doctors in the allocation of scarce resources which can mean and certainly did mean some short time ago a differential equality of access, for example to renal dialysis, depending on where one lived.

Such an approach would, therefore, imply that we were funding the person and his or her health needs rather than the institution. Institutions in the public and private sectors would then compete for these resource rights. The proposal I am making would secure a clear kind of entitlement, although, as in other spheres including negative rights, it would fall short of some kind of complete or absolute entitlement to provision. As I have argued, however, the latter is not a very meaningful notion. Seeing welfare in this sort of way could encourage a sense of empowerment among consumers of services which is secured to them although not to institutions in non-market ways. In a certain way too it could mitigate the sense of dependency which both the Right and the Left now accept has been a feature of bureaucratically provided public services. If individuals have a clearer view of their entitlements within state services, or state-regulated private services, they will in a real sense come to have more power within those services.

Rights of Citizenship

Rights of citizenship can be an important counterpart to the power which the consumer has in the market. This is particularly important if one accepts at least some of the public choice critique of government-provided or government-regulated services. On the whole, neo-liberals take the view that the only solution to the problems posed by public choice theory is to try to replace state-provided services by market-based provision. Private provision, they argue, makes the bureaucracy or professional group responsive to the customer which is not possible within the public services. However, as I argued earlier, there are major defects in this approach and if we are to have a set of state-provided services, as we clearly must in health, education, welfare, and in services such as the police, then citizen empowerment within them might well be an alternative way forward. It is also a more plausible way forward in my view than the usual solution to the same problem proposed on the Left: that bureaucracies and professionals should in some way be made democratically accountable. While there is no doubt a role for democratic accountability at the macro level it means very little to the individual consumer of state services, particularly when the legislation providing for those services, whether these are for health or for the police, do not yield any individual rights or entitlements. Having a set of entitlements would be an alternative to democratisation which in any case has very severe limits in the public choice literature.

The Nature of Entitlements

The nature of the entitlements would also set clear performance indicators for providers of the service which would be more transparent and would not be determined by the producers themselves. One clear example is in education where the provision of the national curriculum could then be seen as an entitlement, with redress if the school fails to provide it. If entitlement is combined with limited-term contracts for producers, it could be a powerful mechanism for ensuring that such performance indicators are adhered to. Here I would include producers such as the police as much as health and educational providers. If we had a more transparent set of such performance indicators, which could be developed through democratic discussion, as well as limited tenure for chief constables and consultants, there might be more pressure to ensure that such performance indicators are met. This is to some degree already happening in the universities. Each university department is at this moment being assessed in terms of its research; if the last exercise was anything to go by, individuals who have a nil return for research when they have a contractual obligation to undertake it will come under great pressure to take early retirement or improve performance.

An approach of this sort, which would embody a more explicit contractual relationship between the providers of services and those who are paying for them, might well provide a better way forward in securing clearer performance tests in the public sector. Some years ago Peter Hain[1] argued that if a local council failed to provide a tenant with a repair to a council house during a given period, then the tenant should have a right to have the repair done privately and bill the council. This sort of means of exit from the existing form of service should be made available within those parts of the public sector where it is possible and where the performance falls below the indicated level. This would be feasible in both the educational and the health sectors where exit could be to other public providers such as other schools or to more efficient health districts. It cannot apply to the police because of its monopoly of local services. However, as I have suggested, one could develop performance indicators here and link the renewal of the contracts of chief constables and perhaps other senior officers who manage police forces to the achievement of such indicators.

In my view such an approach would provide an additional and, I suspect, a better way of keeping public services up to the mark than yet more layers of bureaucracy such as the schools inspectorate, the inspectorate of constabulary, or the health inspectorate which the Labour Party is proposing at the moment. It would also allow a more sensible discussion of the internal form of provision within state-provided services. Bench-marks of service delivery, involving some sort of consensual level of resource provision together with equality of access to such provision, would enable the questions of whether there should be internal markets within the NHS, or whether there might be some scope for vouchers in education or child care as Patricia Hewitt has recently argued in *New*

[1] Peter Hain, *The Democratic Alternative*, London: Penguin Books, 1984.

Socialist,[1] to be examined empirically rather than as matters of principle. If entitlements to services embodying standards seem to be ways of delivering services more effectively within the two constraints which a theory of rights would yield, then they would be worth considering, particularly if they embodied some kind of redistributive element, which, as I have argued against the neo-liberal view, should remain an essential ingredient of public policy.

Conclusion

In conclusion, I believe that a politics of citizenship and rights is a vital ingredient of modern welfare provision and could provide a very important counterpart to the market-based, consumerist approach adopted almost in its entirety by the present administration. If we are interested in empowering all people in society this has to be done certainly by the market, but cannot be done wholly by it. We still require state-provided or state-guaranteed services. But we on the Left should not try to reinvent yesterday and go back to forms of welfare institutions which, with the best intentions, actually put very little power in the hands of those they were designed to help.

---

[1] Patricia Hewitt, *New Socialist*, No. 60, 1989, p. 9.

Part 2

Markets, Citizenship and the Welfare State: Some Critical Reflections

Norman Barry

The Author

Norman Barry is Professor of Politics at the University of Buckingham and Visiting Scholar at the Social Philosophy and Policy Center, Bowling Green State University, Ohio, for the academic year 1989—1990. He has published widely in the areas of political philosophy and political economy. His books include *Hayek's Social and Economic Philosophy* (1979), *An Introduction to Modern Political Theory* (1981; second edition 1989) and *The New Right* (1987). He is a regular contributor to the IEA journal, *Economic Affairs*, and is the author of a Hobart Paper, *The Invisible Hand in Economics and Politics* (1988). His latest book, *Welfare*, is to be published by the Open University Press in 1990. This paper was written while the author was at the Social Philosophy and Policy Center, Bowling Green State University, Ohio. He is grateful to the institution for its excellent research facilities.

Introduction

During the last ten years the welfare state has come under increasing critical scrutiny; not only from writers fundamentally opposed to its economic and ethical foundations but also from social theorists favourable to its aims. The latter, however, have been forced into a rather defensive position in response to the political and intellectual revival of liberal individualist ideas,[1] and their admitted intellectual power, and because of the dissatisfaction they themselves evinced at the way existing welfare systems work. Although much of the debate was fuelled by the post-1973 slow-down in economic growth experienced by Western democracies as a result of the oil crisis, and the fear that pre-existing levels of state expenditure on welfare were unsustainable, it is clear that there is more to the problem than this. For one thing, Western democracies have maintained levels of spending, in real terms, on welfare, despite the adverse economic conditions of the late 1970s and early 1980s. For another, it has become clear that the argument about the welfare state is fundamentally about values, and for that reason has been conducted independently of ephemeral economic events. Many aspects of the welfare debate, though not all, cannot be discussed in terms of evidence only.

Principles of Welfare

The values on which the welfare state are normally said to be founded comprise altruism, an expanded notion of human rights, an objective criterion of need and, in more recent times, citizenship. As I shall attempt to show, these values are often vague and indecisive in their application to public policy, they do not form a well-structured whole but are often in conflict with each other, and do not always validate morally

---

[1] Green, D., *The New Right*, Brighton: Harvester, 1987; Barry, N.P., *The New Right*, London: Croom Helm, 1987.

the institutional form of the welfare state with which we are familiar. Indeed, the protean nature of welfare philosophy is sadly reflected in the variety (and often incoherence) of forms in which welfare institutions and policies appear. Some typical welfare institutions, a spectacular example is zero-priced university education, are carried out almost in defiance of the egalitarian aims of welfare philosophy. Exposure of counter-productive welfare policy has featured strongly in contemporary criticisms of the welfare state.

Nevertheless, however disparate the underlying principles of welfare may be they do take on a semblance of coherence when they are used to criticise the doctrine of classical liberalism. The idea of the welfare *state* itself invites an obvious comparison between the market and the state. For although the standard 'market versus state' argument is now a little *passé* (it is hard even to conceive a society that has completely eliminated either) the question of the relative influence each should have in social life, and the ethical principles upon which their respective roles are founded, is of paramount importance to the discussion of welfare.

The Concept of Welfare —
A Classical-Liberal Approach

This distinction goes to the heart of the meaning of the concept of welfare. Market philosophers, drawing upon the tradition of liberal economics, understand welfare in terms of individual *subjective* and private experiences.[1] The most obvious indication of this well-being is in the free and voluntary choices expressed normally in the market-place: though it should be stressed that such voluntarism is not confined to the market; there are other possibilities of free action such as charitable donations. What this approach does emphasise, however, is the anti-paternalism of classical liberal theory and

---

[1] James Buchanan has expressed this view the most forcibly; see especially his *The Limits of Liberty*, Chicago: University of Chicago Press, 1975.

its reluctance to concede the point that welfare can have any meaning detached from individual experiences. Thus the two fundamental propositions of liberal welfare theory are: first, that each individual is the best judge of his own welfare, and second, that social welfare can only be legitimately said to increase if everybody's welfare increases (or, at least, if one person's welfare increases while others remain unaffected). Implicit in this is a prohibition on the interpersonal comparison of utilities, i.e. it is not possible for an external observer to compare the well-being of individuals affected by various courses of action.[1] Thus from this point it follows that a policy, say progressive income tax, which made some people better off while harming others, even a minority and then only minutely, could not be said to enhance social welfare.

This austere account of welfare is obviously derived from the elementary model of two-person exchange found in liberal economics. Part of its austerity as a welfare judgement is a consequence of the attempt to restrict value judgements to the minimum and to keep welfare statements within the realm of 'scientific' economics. This is perhaps ambitious since all of the propositions above are inherently contentious. It is, for example, by no means self-evidently true that people are the best judges of their own welfare. However that may be, the point of this approach to the current debate is that it confines propositions about welfare to preferences: because preferences emanate from subjective choice they are accorded higher priority than 'needs'. The latter are either regarded as reducible to preferences or as expressive of some paternalist judgement about other people's well-being made by political authorities (or, indeed, collectivist welfare economists).

It does not follow from this theory that, because welfare is limited to preference satisfaction, there is no role for a welfare state. It is agreed by most liberal individualists, with the

---

[1] That it is possible to make such comparisons has been a standard feature of utilitarian political economy since Jeremy Bentham (1748–1832).

exception of anarcho-capitalists and extreme libertarians, that preferences can be legitimately expressed through the political process as well as the market mechanism. On the assumption that there are such things as public goods, i.e. wanted goods, such as defence, law and order, and clean air, that cannot be supplied by the market, there is no *a priori* reason to exclude from the public realm people's subjective preferences for welfare. It is maintained, of course, that the democratic choice mechanism reflects this rather inefficiently, that people's preferences for the relief of indigence are not actually met in the existing structure of welfare services. Nevertheless, once it is conceded that a state exists legitimately for the realisation of preferences, welfare cannot be excluded. It can only be so excluded if the state is limited exclusively to the protection of negative rights, as it is in Robert Nozick's political philosophy.[1]

'Compulsory Altruism'

The conventional, and not altogether satisfactory, argument for some sort of compulsory welfare state consistent with individualist moral principles is that people's private preferences for the relief of indigence come up against familiar public good problems, i.e. the difference that one person's charity makes is so small that he has no incentive to contribute. Therefore, everybody would be made better off by a form of 'compulsory altruism'.[2] Despite this, the individualist will still argue that the possibility that eleemosynary activity can at least partially solve the welfare problem should not be entirely discounted.

Although some rationale can be found for public welfare within liberal individualism it has to be conceded that it is a doctrine that makes the relief of suffering depend entirely upon the existence of generosity; a sentiment of altruism which is expressed either through voluntary action or through

---

[1] Robert Nozick, *Anarchy, State and Utopia*, Oxford: Blackwell, 1974.

[2] For a refutation of this argument, see Sugden, R., *Who Cares?*, London: Institute of Economic Affairs, 1984.

a precarious and unreliable electoral mechanism. Because individuals are defined atomistically as preference maximisers they can have no welfare claims that might derive from their membership of a community, or from a notion of citizenship that extends beyond the equal rights that obtain in a system of just laws, or even from the sheer fact of need itself except without qualifications.

A Residual Service

Even when the welfare state is not made to depend exclusively on people's preferences it remains no more than a residual service: indeed, it has even been justified, especially in the nineteenth century, on the ground that it is necessary in order to prevent social disorder. Hence, much of the classical liberal contribution to the welfare debate is of a negative kind: critical analyses of prevailing institutions and policies involving the use of standard social science methodology, most often derived from economics. However, it cannot be denied that much of this criticism has been devastating. It is here that the meagre assumption of man as a preference-maximiser has turned out to be extraordinarily useful in the *causal* analysis of the effects of various welfare policies. As I shall show below, the existence of easily available welfare has a well-documented tendency to encourage the preference for welfare over work. The descriptive properties of *homo economicus* seem depressingly resistant to the claims that a widespread welfare state will generate a different kind of citizen from that which inhabits market society. However, the difference that the discoveries of social science make to the normative welfare theory (perhaps it does not matter that easily available welfare generates dependency?) is itself a complex issue and can only be explored through an analysis of specific welfare institutions and policies. By normative welfare theory it is meant that set of extra-market principles which is used to justify intervention by the state to relieve indigence, provide welfare services such as education, health care, housing and so on, or to generate equality for its own sake.

The Interventionist Approach to Social Welfare

The conventional interventionist and non-liberal approach to social welfare differs fundamentally from the above. It is not that it is necessarily non-individualist in a methodological sense (although it is true that some social welfare theorists do claim that the collective delivery of certain services has a collective value that cannot be factored down to individual experiences) that distinguishes the interventionist but rather the rejection of the claim that the notion of welfare is exhausted by preference or want satisfaction. There are genuine needs which the market does not always meet. However, the contemporary social welfare theorist, with some exceptions of diminishing influence, does not reject the market entirely: the exchange mechanism is recognised as a welfare-maximising device that is superior to a centrally planned society in generating economic prosperity. Neither is there much sympathy with Marxism: indeed there cannot be, since typical welfare institutions and policies are designed on the assumption that private property and capitalism will continue, in defiance of the Marxist and historicist prediction of their inevitable demise.

The major argument of social welfare theory is that the individualist account of well-being is deficient precisely because it neglects, or ignores, those claims and entitlements that are grounded in moral claims other than market exchanges or gifts. In addition to the self-assumed obligations that occur in contractual relationships enforced by common rules, there are other, equally compelling duties that we have to the deprived, whatever the *cause* of their deprivation, as citizens of an organised community. Indeed, some social welfare theorists argue that market relationships, if uncorrected by the state, are often the cause of such deprivation. Irrespective of this, the basic point is that want satisfaction, even if it were the major defining characteristic of welfare, is morally subordinate to need satisfaction.

If the liberal ideal of a pluralistic society, in which individuals pursue a variety of ends, is to have a universal appeal it cannot sanction morally a situation in which certain individuals are more or less permanently disabled because of their lack of resources. In attempting to drive a wedge between needs and wants, Raymond Plant argues that: 'Basic needs have to be satisfied to do anything at all'.[1] In a similar vein, Alan Gewirth[2] maintains that his 'principle of generic consistency' (a method of establishing the validity of moral values by correct reasoning from incontrovertible premisses) requires that there must be legitimate welfare claims because without them individuals would lack a necessary ingredient of human action — a level of well-being. These are in effect attempts to attack liberal anti-welfarism on its own grounds.

Welfare Entitlements

What these, and other similar arguments, amount to is the claim that individuals have welfare entitlements as compelling as those that accrue legitimately from free contracts; and that these entitlements recognise needs that have a claim to satisfaction prior to wants. Such entitlements, vague though they are, are enforceable and therefore do not depend on generosity or beneficence. Although few social welfare theorists would claim that the onus of need satisfaction lies exclusively on the state, the strong implication is that the state must be the primary agent for this. It is this line of reasoning that attempts to show that people are citizens not just market traders, and that this citizenship necessitates something more

---

[1] 'Needs, Agency and Rights', in Sampford, C. and Galligan, D.J., (eds), *Law, Rights and The Welfare State*, London: Croom Helm, 1986.
[2] *Reason and Morality*, Chicago: University of Chicago Press, 1978.

than the equal protection of the laws. What it does is to reintroduce the idea of status into social and political theory.

Thus the whole panoply of ethical theory — social justice, rights, needs, equality, and so on — is used to buttress this key notion of citizenship. It is also usual for the social welfare school to try to show that the market and its inevitable inequalities in some way causes distress, which the state has a duty of relieving.

Moral Objections to the Market

The market is morally condemnable in at least two ways. First, despite its admitted virtues, an uncorrected market will generate pockets of unemployment, low wages and even destitution, largely because the restless change it generates will produce innocent victims: people rendered 'unfree' or deprived not by actions attributable to particular individuals but by the very anonymity of the exchange process. A related point is that a market system operating within a regime of unequal resources will simply replicate those inequalities in a kind of genetic manner. Implicit in all this is the argument that the market in practice does not 'make everyone better off', that the prosperity of the better endowed does not trickle down to the poorest.

The second objection to the market is addressed perhaps not quite so much to the exchange process itself but more to the moral (or amoral) attitudes it generates. This point is particularly relevant to tragedies that affect people randomly; being born with devastating physiological and mental disadvantages is perhaps the most obvious example. Of course, many of the vicissitudes of life can be coped with via the market principle of insurance, but some clearly cannot. It would be absurd to blame markets *directly* for genetic catastrophes but the argument is that, since the exchange mechanism is powered by self-interest, this psychological motivation attenuates our moral sense and displaces that notion of altruism which a civilised society requires. This is clearly what Richard Titmuss had in mind when he wrote of the blood donor as the model of an altruistic citizen

> In not asking or expecting any payment of money those donors signified their belief in the willingness of other men to act altruistically in the future, and to combine together to make a gift freely should they have a need for it.[1]

A moral theory which considers that the only binding obligations are those that are voluntarily assumed, and regards other duties as merely supererogatory (desirable but not enforceable) is, he claimed, unlikely to encourage a caring, civilised society. Once again, the market undermines a more expansive notion of citizenship.

The 'Welfare' State?

However, what is rarely considered by the social welfare school is the possibility that the existence of widespread public welfare arrangements may be, at least in part, a causal factor in the perpetuation of social problems and in the failure to generate good citizenship. This is as much, if not more so, a difficulty for traditional individualist solutions to the problem of the relief of indigence, i.e. cash redistribution to the poor unencumbered by social obligations, as it is for typical 'welfare state' techniques that involve the delivery of welfare goods in kind (housing, health care, education and so on). For in both approaches the real demands of well-being may not be addressed. That is, the public provision of welfare (especially when individuals come to depend on it almost exclusively), in whatever form it is delivered, may not be conducive to a person's well-being where that is understood to encompass something more than the satisfactions derived from income or from a zero-priced service. The notions of self-esteem,

---

[1] *The Gift Relationship*, London: Allen & Unwin, 1970, p. 175.

autonomy and personal independence are highly pertinent to this conception of well-being.

What is also crucially important is the connection between the normative theory of social welfare and the actual structure of institutions and policies in existing welfare states. It is important to know *what* welfare state the welfare philosophers are defending. Not only are existing welfare states acknowledged (even by their principled defenders) to be characterised by inefficiency and inequity, with many of their benefits *not* going to the people for whom they were intended, but the principles on which they are founded are of such a heterogeneous nature that they have few unequivocal policy implications. Of course, such practical difficulties do not affect the validity of the alleged right to welfare if that is merely being philosophically demonstrated. However, it is still incumbent on welfare theorists to consider the connection between the right to welfare and the institutional arrangements that are supposed to guarantee it. This is especially important in view of the fact that welfare claims may be in conflict with other values held by welfare theorists; notably the democratic imperative. That lack of compassion which is alleged to characterise the exchange relationship is just as likely to be present in the voting process: the removal of the market from certain areas of social life does not necessarily mean the removal of selfishness.

A further tension within welfare theory is that between the welfare claims made on behalf of men *qua* men and those made on their behalf as citizens of particular communities. Some welfare philosophers are overtly universalist, i.e. they claim that there are rights to well-being that hold across cultural boundaries. This can be taken to extremes: as in the slightly absurd right to 'holidays with pay' solemnly specified in the United Nations Declaration of Human Rights (1948).[1]

---

[1] For a critique see Maurice Cranston, *What are Human Rights?*, London: The Bodley Head, 1973.

The alarming international redistributive implications of such welfare claims have led not surprisingly to concentration on those that pertain to particular communities. However, it should be remembered that any welfare (and hence redistributive) theory that relies on claims generated by general features of the human condition runs up against this problem. One possible, and certainly plausible, suggestion is that the duties we owe to the deprived in the rest of the world are supererogatory while those that are owed to the citizens of a particular community are compelling. But one is entitled to ask why the deprived of developed nations should be so privileged by a philosophy so concerned with the meeting of needs and with the propagation of the altruistic sentiment? The reason is the special importance that is attached to the concept of citizenship in welfare theory.

Citizenship

At a first glance citizenship refers to a certain kind of exclusivity: someone is a citizen of a country because he has certain legal protections and entitlements that do not apply to outsiders. It is clearly a much more formal concept than a related notion, 'community', that appears frequently in welfare philosophy. Although the two concepts are sometimes used interchangeably in the normative theory of welfare, community is a vague, and rather romantic, notion that confers identity on people through the common ties of language and culture. It is not at all clear what this might imply for welfare theory, since the varieties of communities to which individuals may belong within political boundaries do not in a realistic way sum to a corporate entity which expresses a common purpose, i.e. a collective enterprise that might be used to ground extra-market payments to the needy.[1] Community is also a much

---

[1] For a sceptical view of community from welfare philosophers, see Plant, R., Lesser, H. and Taylor-Gooby, P., *Political Philosophy and Social Welfare*, London: Routledge, 1980, Chapter 9. This particular chapter was written by Raymond Plant.

more exclusive idea than citizenship because membership of a community is 'natural', often founded upon a common language, rather than artificial; indeed, the promotion of a rigid communitarian ideal has a tendency to discount the welfare claims of those outside the natural unit.

This is not to deny that voluntary welfare provision is a feature of communities (indeed, sceptics of the welfare state often claim that its functions could be better performed by communities) but only to suggest that communitarianism does not capture the major elements of modern welfare philosophy. For the latter has its roots in at least a variant of liberal theory: the idea that 'abstract' man, unencumbered by communal affiliations, has certain 'entitlements' and guaranteed freedoms to pursue his subjective ends, irrespective of the demands of a dubious common good. What differentiates social welfare theory from traditional classical liberalism is the argument that these entitlements are radically incomplete without a strong element of redistribution: claims to resources which are as compelling as claims to legal protection. If there is any one normative principle that unites all the otherwise heterogeneous welfare philosophies it is that a genuine liberal society is impossible without legally guaranteed conditions of well-being.

'Citizenship and Social Class'

The most persuasive and coherent of citizenship theories is that of T.H. Marshall; indeed, contemporary welfare doctrines may be seen as footnotes to his fundamental ideas. In a famous essay, *Citizenship and Social Class*, first published in 1949,[1] Marshall proposed a theory of citizenship which rejected the Marxist idea of inevitable class conflict, and the concomitant notion that the state must inevitably oppress non-owners of capital (who are, in effect, 'subjects') on behalf of owners.

---

[1] Reprinted in *Class, Citizenship and Social Development*, New York: Doubleday, 1964.

In his view, citizenship, when completed with welfare entitlements, was an integrating force which softened the impact of class struggle and indeed blurred the edges of social divisions. The institutions of the welfare state achieve this by incorporating social rights into the status of citizenship, 'thus creating a universal right to real income which is not proportionate to the market value of the claimant.'[1]

This is the canonical theory of the welfare state: the demonstration of a legal entitlement to welfare which, although modifying the random income distribution of the market, must be seen as complementary to liberal capitalism rather than hostile to it. In Marshall's explanation, the development of claims to specific welfare services is overtly evolutionary. The welfare rights implicit in full citizenship were preceded by the growth of civil rights and equality before the law (which emerged out of a medieval society based on status), followed by the establishment of political rights through the extension of the franchise in the nineteenth and twentieth centuries.

Welfare Rights and Social Theory

Marshall's argument is partly instrumental, i.e. capitalism could not survive without a welfare component, and partly moral, in that welfare entitlements are implicit within the liberal ideal of equality. His ethical position is to be sharply distinguished from that of Richard Titmuss. For Titmuss saw the exchange relationship itself as destructive of social solidarity and the altruistic impulse: 'Capitalism is a biological failure: it is promoting the extinction of society.'[2] By assimilating the welfare rights of citizenship to the liberal tradition, and indeed evincing a not inconsiderable approval of a corrected market order, Marshall showed himself to be a more realistic theorist

---

[1] *Ibid.*, p. 96.
[2] Quoted by Kincaid, J., in his essay, 'Titmuss', in Barker, P. (ed), *Founders of the Welfare State*, London: Heinemann, 1984, p. 116.

of the welfare state tradition than those in the Titmuss school. The latter, by founding welfare almost exclusively on altruism are, in effect, forced to rely on the state for the expression of this sentiment whenever it has been suppressed by selfish market motivations: a somewhat precarious position to hold. Indeed, there is a reluctance in Titmuss to concede the importance of rights. Since they are too redolent of adversarial relationships, he would replace them by the discretion of benevolent officials.

However, the claim that welfare rights have the same cognitive force as other liberal rights has still to be justified. Marshall's implicit argument that evolution somehow validates them is clearly not good enough, though it has some force against the more extreme Marxist anti-welfare state arguments. To say that the welfare state has evolved is surely not to say that it is 'right' without falling foul of some orthodox and compelling philosophical objections to the possibility of deriving normative statements from purely factual ones. After all, the demand for welfare would not be invalidated merely by a (hypothetically) successful Thatcherite erosion of welfare provision.[1] Again, classical liberals might maintain that the emergence of the welfare state was largely the result of strategic electoral pressure, or sheer political serendipity, rather than the expression of an evolving moral ideal. It could also be argued that the increasing prosperity of capitalist society should gradually *reduce* the range of welfare rights.

Citizenship and Needs

The more popular argument for welfare rights is derived from the concept of 'need': for this suggests that there are certain necessary conditions for full citizenship which are not met by purely market arrangements. To the extent that the market attends only to wants, not only will the deprived be excluded

---

[1] Desmond King and Jeremy Waldron, 'Citizenship, Social Citizenship and the Defence of Welfare Provision', *British Journal of Political Science*, 18, 1988, p. 424.

but even if some redistributive 'cash' device were granted to them it does not follow that it would be spent in such a way as to be conducive to citizenship. For the welfare state in this theory must involve 'specific' egalitarianism, i.e. the more or less equal provision of education, health, unemployment benefit, and so on. Citizenship requires that individuals be active and informed members of the community, capable of taking on its burdens as well as enjoying its benefits. As Marshall noted: 'we have here a personal right combined with a public duty to exercise the right'.[1] For this reason, the citizenship school is surely right to reject that welfare state (no matter how generous) associated with Milton Friedman: it would convert all welfare state provisions into cash payments untied to any 'desirable' form of expenditure.[2] For this would place too great an emphasis on mere choice and provide no guarantee that its exercise would eventuate in desirable civic virtues.

But to give any force to the argument, the priority of needs over wants has to be established. The rationale of the welfare state as we know it depends on there being objective needs which it, and only it, can address. There must be a range of objective needs different from the wants that may be expressed in the market, otherwise the welfare state would be simply a cash transfer system and its ideology indistinct from purely individualistic classical liberalism. Yet if it is true that needs are distinct from wants, and that their satisfaction is an overriding priority, then the welfare problem has little at all to do with choice. The welfare state becomes then an entirely paternalist system, with authorities (elected or otherwise) deciding what are objective needs. Of course, some element of paternalism is inevitable in the welfare state, but an important criticism is that its organisation precludes choice, especially in education and medicine, and places too much discretion in the

---

[1] *Class, Citizenship and Social Development, op. cit.*, p. 82.
[2] See Friedman's *Capitalism and Freedom*, Chicago: University of Chicago Press, 1962.

hands of its officials. Yet one of the major claims of 'liberal' welfare state theory is to reduce discretion to the minimum. There is a conflict in citizenship theory between the liberal demand for want satisfaction and the welfarist imperative that objective needs be met.

Needs or Wants?

There is, however, a fundamental difficulty in distinguishing between needs and wants.[1] It is, of course, true in a trivial sense that somebody can be objectively in need of something without overtly expressing a want for it: an obvious example would be some particular medical treatment which is required for a person's survival even though he may be unaware of it. But this is clearly a *conditional* need, a disguised want for health care, shared by all people. Presumably education is a similar conditional need, necessary for the satisfaction of a want for a higher income, or merely required for the pleasurable experience of enjoying knowledge for its own sake.

There is a strong case for suggesting that all needs are in reality disguised wants and that there are no objective needs that take precedence over wants. The admission of a special category of needs could lead to the obliteration of the market economy by a needs-meeting state. The needs, for example, for companionship and sex are not entirely frivolous yet would one seriously contemplate the possibility of the state meeting them? If the proposed analytical separation is not possible then obviously the priority of needs over wants is unsustainable and one of the rationales of the welfare state would fail. The state would be faced with the embarrassing, and fundamentally illiberal task of selecting from the whole range of wants those presumed to be of special significance. This is not to deny the reality of pressing 'needs' but only to suggest that

---

[1] See Goodin, R., *Reasons for Welfare*, Princeton, NJ: Princeton University Press, 1988, Chapter 2, for a thorough analysis of needs and wants. Also, Baybrooke, D., *Meeting Needs*, Princeton, NJ: Princeton University Press, 1987, for an overly complex attempt to establish objective criteria of needs.

the concept is not adequate to determine uncontroversially the respective roles of the market and the state.

Citizenship and 'Specific Egalitarianism'

So, far from being 'objective', needs turn out to be infinitely contestable. But even if there were agreement on a separate category of needs there is still the difficulty of establishing some priority rule for ordering the competing demands within it. How much state expenditure should go on education, in comparison with, say, health care or housing, is an impossible question to answer once the allocative mechanism of the market has been removed. The electoral process, surely an imperfect surrogate for this, is unlikely to produce outcomes that cohere with the realisation of the supposed objective needs. A further point is the Herculean task faced by administrators if they are to be entrusted with the role of determining what these needs are in particular cases. The 'knowledge' question posed by a centralised welfare system nicely parallels similar intractable problems faced by central planners trying to organise the production and distribution of wanted goods and services in the absence of prices in a *dirigiste* economy.[1]

I suspect that the rationale for the welfare state does not depend on the invocation of unmet needs as a special category of human demands but on the more tractable claim that in a market society uncorrected by state intervention some individuals will simply be left without those resources that are required to make citizenship meaningful. This severs that *necessary* link between citizenship and specific egalitarianism (welfare in the form of particular services based on need), although it does not exclude it. However, a theory that attended to want satisfaction rather than the meeting of objective needs would have the added advantage of reducing that *discretion* which seems to be such a part of existing

---

[1] See Lavoie, D., *Rivalry and Central Planning*, Cambridge: Cambridge University Press, 1985.

welfare states. Nevertheless, the precise form of welfare that citizenship requires, either in cash or in kind, is particularly difficult to deduce unambiguously from welfare theory.

Justifying Welfare in Citizenship Theory: Citizenship and Political Order

The resource claims that emanate from citizenship theory would appear to have at least three possible justifications. One arising out of the social disintegration and alienation that might occur in the absence of welfare, another out of a genuine claim based on rights and a third out of the demand for equality itself.

The argument here is that without resources a citizen would be denied that sense of belonging that a stable community requires; indeed large numbers of people, alienated because of their distress, could very well constitute a threat to its integrity. Curiously enough, this argument echoes some rather disturbing opinions that were uttered in the early part of the nineteenth century when 'outdoor relief' to unemployed able-bodied labourers was justified because of the belief that these people could constitute a revolutionary threat.[1] Historically, such relief, especially under the Poor Law, was accompanied by a loss of civil rights. Nowadays, the argument is part of the 'civic humanist' or 'republican' ideal that understands a society as more than a collection of anonymous individuals held together by abstract rules of law: it is a community of active, participating citizens. Such a conception would, of course, preclude the possibility that the grant of welfare should be accompanied by a loss of civil rights.[2]

---

[1] See Fraser, D., *The Evolution of the British Welfare State*, London: Macmillan, 1973.
[2] King and Waldron, *op. cit.*, p. 421.

'Good Citizenship'

It is really a quasi-empirical (but rather indeterminate) argument whether extensive welfare arrangements produce the requisite social commitment, even if the communitarian ideal were incontrovertibly desirable. There is no evidence that crime or social disorder is much affected by the presence or absence of welfare. If there is a tendency it might well be the other way: reported crime rates were lower in the Depression of the 1930s, and certainly the existence of a black underclass in the US, which consists largely of welfare beneficiaries and which appears to be very much out of step with traditional American values, bodes ill for the hypothesised link between welfare and good citizenship.

The 'good citizenship' argument seems to come up against one of the oldest problems of social science — the 'public good' trap. There are certain activities which are of benefit to everyone but which require the co-operation of all for their delivery; a co-operation which is unlikely to occur because each individual is uncertain about the behaviour of others. It is the reason for the coercive supply of defence, clean air, law and order and so on, and indeed has been used by classical liberals for the delivery of some public welfare. It applies to citizenship, too. For although it is necessary for the ideals of community spirit and solidarity that each citizen should participate in public affairs, vote on non-selfish grounds and most importantly, not exploit welfare for his own advantage, there is no incentive for each person to be so virtuous. Those 'constants' of human nature stressed by David Hume and Adam Smith, primarily self-interest, are as noticeable in the public sphere as in the private. The fact that individuals are not 'moralised' by the existence of welfare is attested to by the fact that conditions are usually imposed on those who receive it. One of the most important messages of Charles Murray's book on the American welfare system is that it is not so much the value of the various welfare benefits that is crucial in their increased take-up but the *relaxation* of the conditions for their receipt.[1] There is as much evidence to show that individuals behave in the manner of *homo economicus*, rather than that of the good citizen, when offered favourable welfare benefits.

Citizenship and Rights

A less flaccid argument for welfare, and one more consonant with the pluralist liberal tradition, understands it as a right to resources morally (and logically) equivalent to the right to non-interference, which we all have, from the invasive actions of the others. It is claimed that just as my well-being is harmed by aggressive action, it is undermined by a lack of resources. Thus the claim to welfare is not validated on citizenship grounds where those refer to some instrumental value but is embedded in a notion of what it is to be an autonomous agent.[2]

The familiar objections to this assimilation of welfare rights to (negative) rights of forbearance are as follows: negative rights do not require positive action by the state, there is a doubt upon whom the duty to meet welfare rights lies, and welfare rights cannot be universalised without violating other equally valuable rights, e.g. the right to property. Classical liberals have often claimed that it is a perversion of the idea of a right to attach it indiscriminately to welfare demands since this implies that there are as many rights as there are demands, i.e. a virtually unlimited number.

In this particular form these objections are not as decisive as they were once thought to be. The most important point is that even negative rights are not costless, for they require possibly expensive state action (hence some inevitable redistribution of resources) for their protection. A clear asymmetry between welfare rights and negative rights would then hold

---

[1] *Losing Ground: American Social Policy 1950–80*, New York: Basic Books, 1984.
[2] Plant, 'Needs, Agency & Rights', *loc. cit.*

only if the latter were interpreted as simply the formal right to forbearance from aggressive action on the part of others with no *positive* duties being imposed on anyone to protect them: a somewhat precarious position to hold (except for the dogged anarcho-capitalist) since a right without protection is hardly a right worth having. This conceptual similarity would seem to hold despite the significant difference in costs between enforcing the basic right to protection and the potentially unlimited welfare rights claims. But even this is to leave aside the question of whether welfare rights can be claimed by all rational agents or whether they are confined to citizens of particular countries.

There is, however, still a conceptual difference between the two rights that is worth stressing: a point that almost all theorists of welfare rights stress is that such a right requires some positive action on the part of its possessor. Thus Gewirth, who certainly believes in the symmetry of negative and positive rights, argues that the agent

> cannot rationally demand of other persons that they help him to have basic well-being unless his own efforts to have it have been unavailing.[1]

David Harris, a proponent of culturally limited social rights rather than universal rights, similarly argues that

> The fact of need, independently of how the need was created, does not provide a sufficient ground upon which a normative defence of need-meeting policy can be founded.[2]

These surely plausible qualifications on welfare rights possession are consistent with a citizenship theory of the type described by Marshall but they surely attenuate its individualis-

---

[1] 'Private Philanthropy and Positive Rights', in Paul, E.F., Miller, Jr., F.D., Paul, J. and Ahrens, J., (eds), *Beneficence, Philanthropy and the Public Good*, Oxford: Blackwell, 1987, p. 68.
[2] *Justifying State Welfare*, Oxford: Blackwell, 1987, pp. 160-1.

tic credentials. However, we would not say that the negative rights of forbearance similarly depended upon the performance of some worthy action. For example, a person may be extremely foolish in walking alone late at night, through an area known to be plagued by muggers, but we would not say that his behaviour rendered his right to non-interference nugatory. Unlike traditional negative rights, the validity of welfare rights does seem to depend on the performance by the agent of certain morally worthy actions.

Citizenship Theory and Liberal Individualism

This marks a significant difference between citizenship theory and traditional liberal individualism. The former is not quite an evolutionary development out of the civil and political aspects of liberalism but is suggestive of a radically different vision of the relationship between the citizen and the state: the citizen has positive duties towards government which he does not have under abstract liberalism. In other words, a person cannot have welfare rights and remain as free as he was before he had them. As Marshall says 'Citizenship is a status bestowed on those who are full members of a community'.[1] But that status has its duties.

Thus, Lawrence Mead, in a subtle critique of the American welfare system, argues that its failure resulted from the granting of welfare benefits as rights and entitlements, unaccompanied by corresponding social obligations, to citizens living in an America still characterised by Lockean liberal individualism: a 'private' world which by definition has no overall end-state or social purpose and imposes little in the way of duties on its citizens beyond obedience to the law. However, treating welfare benefits as Lockean entitlements encouraged welfare demands to grow and did little to stimulate socially responsible behaviour. To counter this, Mead finds

---

[1] *Class, Citizenship, op. cit.*, p. 84.

in citizenship theory a philosophical justification for 'workfare': 'work must be treated as a social obligation akin to paying taxes and obeying the law'.[1]

Ironically, then, so far from welfare rights being consistent with an expansion of liberty, as liberal citizenship theory implies, their legally guaranteed existence must mean less freedom of choice to pursue differing life-styles and unconventional values.

Implementing Welfare Rights

There are further problems with welfare rights which have less to do with their philosophical foundation than with their practical implementation. It is true that legal systems may, and do, embody rights to welfare, and may even give them constitutional protection against transient majorities, just as negative rights are so protected, but this positivist affirmation does not necessarily make them feasible social objectives. For one thing it is not clear how the refusal of the state to grant welfare is justiciable in the same way that an invasion of privacy, or an arbitrary legislative or executive act of censorship, could be litigated. Rights to welfare, if given constitutional protection, are bound to be couched in general or vague terms and are therefore certain to be indeterminate. So it is difficult even to conceive of them as effective 'controllers' of government policy. None of this scepticism is meant to preclude the possibility of other constitutional reforms, e.g. those that might be designed to prevent the middle-class 'capture' of the welfare state (a phenomenon discussed later); it merely casts doubt on our ability to formulate purported welfare rights coherently.

The serious problem is surely that the attribution of welfare rights to individuals in the presence of scarcity (a constant feature of the human condition) throws up insoluble distribu-

---

[1] *Beyond Entitlement*, New York: Basic Books, 1985, p. 82.

tional problems. For example, if the right to life is interpreted other than as a protection against unlawful killing and is taken to mean that a claim on medical resources is legitimate (irrespective of payment), it could place impossible burdens on a community. Rapid advances in medical technology now mean that people can be kept alive far longer than in the past, but the attempt to honour an open-minded right to life is certain to be unsuccessful. Social welfare theorists no doubt find it distasteful and immoral that medical care should be rationed by 'price' rather than allocated in accordance with need, but in nationalised health systems a similar (but non-price) rationing occurs. Doctors, in fact, allocate expensive operations and treatment on the basis of crude utilitarian calculations about the potential earning power of various patients.

Again, the universal provision of old-age pensions related to past earnings may be a desirable welfare goal, but this could impose onerous burdens on the younger generations, especially if population declines and the ratio of workers to retirees worsens. This is a special problem for nationalised pension schemes which are not 'funded' properly and depend almost exclusively on tax transfers from current cohorts of workers. How meaningful is the right to a decent standard of living in retirement in such circumstances?

Citizenship and Equality

The third justification for extensive state welfare that is contained within citizenship theory invokes a broadened concept of equality. The equal rights incorporated in the legal notion of citizenship are inadequate, it is claimed, for full participation in the life of a civilised community. It is argued that their coexistence with pockets not only of deprivation but also of substantial inequality of resources throughout the social order gives a superficial moral approval to a fundamentally unjust system. At the very least, it is maintained that the operation of a free market, subject only to abstract rules of law, will simply reproduce or replicate those inequalities that exist at the foundational level,[1] and hence subvert any claims that individualist philosophers make about the openness and fluidity of capitalist societies.

This is not necessarily an argument against the market mechanism as such. It is not often realised that the market is quite an egalitarian device. In theory, under perfect competition the factors of production (labour, land and capital) are paid just that income required to induce them to produce an 'optimum' of wanted goods and services: the inequalities that obtain here are entirely functional, for without them economic society would operate at a lower level of efficiency. Any 'excess' profit, i.e. income over and above that required for efficiency, has in theory been whittled away by competition. Of course, in the real world such a nirvana does not exist, there are entrepreneurial profits and unequal resource endowments, but nevertheless the market process itself, if left undisturbed, shows a tendency towards the equalisation of income, and even the break-up of large resource holdings. A sincere egalitarian should then logically recommend a greater penetration of social life by the market. Some recognition of this point can be detected in the recent resuscitation of the theory of 'market socialism'. However, the influence of the Titmuss school of social welfare, the members of which regard the institution of the market as socially divisive and destructive of the spirit of altruism on which their conception of welfare depends, has historically been decisive. Marshall's concept of citizenship would certainly not exclude a role for the market; only those dysfunctional elements within it that attenuated full citizenship would come under critical scrutiny.

Universal Services

Nevertheless, the goal of equality has traditionally been sought through the imposition of universal facilities in the typical

---

[1] Hoover, K. and Plant, R., *Conservative Capitalism in Britain and the United States*, London: Routledge, 1988, Chapter 10.

welfare services, education, health, unemployment, pensions, housing, and so on, rather than improving the market mechanism, or even equalising what is thought to be a (morally) arbitrary distribution of resource endowments. Indeed, the reluctance to 'target' those individuals and groups specifically in need, irrespective of egalitarian considerations, reflects the persistent influence of the communitarian and 'social solidarity' motif of much social welfare theory. There seems to be something intrinsically valuable in the common consumption of services, even though it is socially wasteful and productive of much functionless inequality.

The fact that the common provision of public services (specific egalitarianism) favours the middle classes had been known for many years (it was even noted by Titmuss) but the publication of Julian Le Grand's *Strategy of Equality*[1] (and later work co-authored with Robert Goodin)[2] gave the first full explanation of the phenomenon of the inegalitarian effects of unpriced welfare services. It is perhaps ironic that both Le Grand and Goodin are firm advocates of the welfare state. In fact, classical liberals had always regarded it as intuitively obvious that if, for example, university education is supplied at more or less zero price, then this must mean that future high earners are being subsidised by low earners.

Le Grand studied a whole range of social welfare programmes, education, housing, health care and transport, which the state supplied in one form or another. All, to varying degrees, displayed a bias of expenditure to the top fifth of the population (in income and expenditure terms) compared to the bottom fifth. Le Grand found some alarming inequities: in health care the ratio was 1:4, in secondary education for pupils over sixteen years it was 1:8, non-university education 3:5, bus subsidies 3:7, university education 5:4, tax subsidies to owner

---

[1] Julian Le Grand *The Strategy of Equality*, London: Allen & Unwin, 1982.
[2] Julian Le Grand and Robert Goodin, *Not Only the Poor*, London: Allen & Unwin, 1987.

occupiers 6:8, and rail subsidies a remarkable 9:8.[1] All of these data point to significant 'beneficial involvement'[2] in state welfare by the middle classes. People have a habit of adjusting their behaviour to new (and favourable) circumstances offered by non-priced services.

Welfare Consumption

As Le Grand has shown, the fact that a public service is available equally to all does not mean that it will be consumed equally: its consumption will depend upon a whole range of factors that will vary across the population. As he says, there is almost a general principle at work:

> Policies involving subsidies whose distribution is dependent upon people's decision to consume the good or use the service favour the better off.[3]

Thus although health care is available equally to all at zero price, it is likely to be consumed more by middle-class individuals because the 'opportunity cost' (what they have to give up in order to consume) is much lower to them than to working-class patients; for example, the salaried middle classes are less likely to lose money from forgone work when they attend a doctor's surgery, whereas a worker paid by the hour will. The system of heavily subsidised higher education is notoriously productive of great inequality, and 'tax expenditures' on housing (in the form of tax relief on mortgage interest) are sources of great inefficiency and inequity. Le Grand reaches the conclusion that, in some cases, it is likely that there would be greater equality if there were no public expenditure on the service concerned: an implicit recognition of the equalising tendencies of the market. The methodology of the social

---

[1] Le Grand, *Strategy of Equality, op. cit.*, Chapters 2-5.
[2] Le Grand and Goodin, *Not Only the Poor, op. cit.*, Chapter 9.
[3] Le Grand, *Strategy of Equality, op. cit.*, p. 46.

sciences seems to be at odds with the normative demands of social welfare theory.

Middle-Class Pressure

Despite the obvious inefficiencies and inequities associated with state welfare services they still have their defenders in the social welfare and citizenship school. One argument is that without middle-class participation the poorest would be even worse off.[1] Apparently, it is the constant middle-class political pressure ('sharp elbows') that keeps up public expenditure from which the poor benefit, almost by accident. This looks like a rather bizarre application of Adam Smith's 'Invisible Hand' thesis (i.e. that individuals, motivated by self-interest, unintentionally bring about a co-ordination of economic activities from which everybody benefits) to welfare provision. It is apparently selfish consumption of education, health and so on by the better off that ensures the survival of the welfare state for the benefit of the poor. Apart from the fact that this has a quite devastating implication for the argument that welfare institutions tap our resources of altruism, the theory is probably false. It is most unlikely that there would be no welfare state without middle-class participation *and* it is the case, empirically, that the middle classes use their 'sharp elbows' to protect services from which they benefit. Le Grand and Goodin claim that in times of reduced government spending it is those activities that have fewest middle-class users that are most adversely affected.[2] This is neither altruism nor good citizenship.

The attempt to impose egalitarian outcomes on an unpromising, and more or less unchanging, human nature is a misguided policy, contributing neither to justice nor welfare. As a recent

---

[1] See O'Higgins, M., 'Egalitarians, Equalities and Welfare Evaluation', *Journal of Social Policy*, 14, 1987, pp. 1-18.

[2] Le Grand and Goodin, *Not Only the Poor, op. cit.*, Chapter 4.

study[1] has shown, there are more or less intractable features of the human condition which generate remarkably similar distributions of income and resources irrespective of differing social and economic conditions. Thus it is quite likely that Le Grand's own favoured egalitarianism, redistribution at the foundational level of resource ownership, would come up against the same problem. A more acceptable approach to welfare might well mean the abandonment of some of the heady ideals of citizenship in favour of targeting those specifically disfavoured, either by lack of resource endowment or by genetic disadvantage: two phenomena which cannot be attributed to the failure of the market. Indeed, a more potent form of citizenship would be one that 'empowered' people, through voucher schemes for education, loans for university education and widened choice for health care. Such policies would be more effective in making individuals autonomous agents than would their participation as citizens in the democratic process.

Classical Liberals and the Welfare State

However, one should not assume that because collective institutions and policies have a disappointing record, theoretical alternatives fare that much better. An examination of the record of classical liberal theory of state welfare is equally depressing. For although classical liberals have provided much of the criticism of the welfare state, and would like to see it reduced, there is nevertheless a theory of compulsory welfare provision in the social thought of writers such as Milton Friedman and Friedrich Hayek. Although it is true that such welfare as they recommend is residual, extra-market payments to which the recipients are not entitled in a strict economic, moral or contractual sense, and therefore not consistent with the ideals of the social welfare theorists, it is none the less

---

[1] Phelps Brown, H., *The Generation of Inequality*, Oxford: Oxford University Press, 1988.

state welfare: unlike extreme libertarians they are not prepared to leave the deprived entirely to charity.

Welfare Provision as an Orthodox Public Good

Milton Friedman has the most distinctive welfare philosophy and it is his suggestions that have been most influential on classical liberal thought and practice.[1] Basically his argument is that the rationale of redistributive welfare can be derived from the elements of individualistic economics. In a famous passage he wrote

> I am distressed by the sight of poverty; I am benefited by its alleviation; the benefits of other people's charity therefore partly accrue to me. To put it differently, we might all of us be willing to contribute to the relief of poverty, provided everyone else did.[2]

In other words, welfare provision is presented as an orthodox public good: something that we all benefit from but which no one has any incentive to provide. It is a rather desperate attempt to incorporate a type of welfare state into orthodox Paretian welfare economics. It is not that there is some demonstrable moral duty to relieve suffering but rather that such relief makes everyone better off. However, it is rather obvious that compulsory welfare is not like other public goods. The voluntary contributions of individuals do make a difference, however small, to the supply of welfare and in this sense welfare is different from, say, defence, law and order, or even clean air. This is not at all to say that the relief of indigence should be left to charity but only to observe that public welfare is not technically a public good. If Friedman's presuppositions are true it is hard to explain why there is any charitable activity at all, and there clearly is.

---

[1] Although Hayek has perhaps the most cogent account of the *theories* of justice and welfare.

[2] Friedman, *Capitalism and Freedom, op. cit.*, p. 190.

A further point is that Friedman depends upon a rather thick spread of the altruistic sentiment across society if his theory is to be at all plausible. In fact, one commentator[1] (at least) has noticed an ironic similarity between his welfare ideals and those of Richard Titmuss: both philosophies depend on the existence of 'anonymous donors' unmotivated by any feeling of reciprocal duty but only by the desire to satisfy the altruistic preference. Yet the welfare state, in whatever form it is delivered, must involve redistribution, which is normally financed by people many of whom, it can be safely assumed, are unwilling. It is a redistributive process that requires justification in ethics: something that the rights and citizenship theorists at least were very much aware of. But Friedman, of course, is an ethical subjectivist.

Cash Benefits

There is, however, a kind of ethic implicit in the way in which Friedman thinks welfare should be delivered, i.e. in the form of cash payments (the famous negative income tax) untied to any specific form of expenditure (although the provision of elementary education in kind might be permitted since, in addition to a surely plausible paternalist argument, it provides the public good of inculcating civic virtues and basic social values). In general, any provision of welfare in kind — health care, housing, higher education and so on — involves the illiberal principle that public authorities are licensed to select certain ends as being especially desirable out of the whole range of ends that feature in a free and pluralist society. To borrow the title of a famous book by Friedman, people should be 'free to choose',[2] and that principle must apply to welfare goods as much as to consumer goods. Indeed, why should

[1] Sugden, *Who Cares?, op. cit.*
[2] Milton and Rose Friedman, *Free to Choose*, London: Secker & Warburg, 1980.

negative income tax beneficiaries spend it on welfare goods, anyway?

Flaws in the 'Cash' Solution

Friedman's solution to the welfare problem is far too neat and elides the problems that inexorably follow from any kind of welfare provision. The major flaw is that it identifies the welfare problem as entirely one of cash: the glib assumption is that 'the problem with the poor is that they do not have enough money'. But as many social commentators have noted, lack of resources is only part of the problem. Questions of personal well-being and self-esteem are equally important: as is the question of *how* people get into poverty in the first place, and *why* that seems to perpetuate itself through the generations. If the problem were simply one of cash, then prosperous Western economies would have solved it long ago; yet the evidence is that the number of people dependent on welfare actually rises *pari passu* with economic growth.

In practice, as Charles Murray discovered,[1] where versions of the negative income tax were tried in two American states, it produced the worst results of all welfare schemes in terms of increased dependence, marital breakdown and defection from work. It is not often realised that Murray's powerful critique of the welfare state is addressed more to the naive versions of classical liberal welfare theory than it is to the more orthodox doctrines.

A further interesting point about the 'cash' solution to welfare problems, and the contrast between it and the various 'in kind' and paternalist theories, is the rather eerie similarity it has with the debate occasioned by the introduction of the New Poor Law in 1834. For this legislation introduced the principle of 'less eligibility' and the 'work-house test' precisely to discourage people from becoming eligible for poor relief.

---

[1] *Losing Ground, op. cit.*, Chapter 11.

The Speenhamland system, which it outlawed, was a version of the negative income tax since it paid a supplement to income, untied to any social condition. Harsh, paternalist and rights-reducing though it was, the New Poor Law was based on what many classical liberals believe to be universal principles of human nature.

Friedman would no doubt claim that his welfare theory is consistent with these principles. Indeed, he has often said that welfare is like any other good or service: if it is offered at zero price the demand will be infinite. However, his presumed solution to the problem of an ever-rising welfare bill — cut the value of the payments — is again too glib. How low would they have to fall to produce the deterrence effect? To subsistence? And if they did fall drastically would not that arbitrarily harm 'innocent people'? In fact, given the vote-maximising processes of democracy, it is quite likely that the cost of the negative income tax would be bid up and the welfare problems would remain.

It is not even clear that the value neutrality that Friedman so much admires, i.e. the idea that no state should impose any particular conception of virtue on its citizens, is actually implied by his own theory. For the 'donors', those taxpayers who fund the negative income tax, are likely to have preferences as to how their money should be spent. Should their possible preference that money should be tied to specific services, such as health care, education, pensions, insurance and so on, be discounted? To do so may well be in the spirit of anti-paternalism, and consistent with the idea that autonomy is coterminous with individual choice, but at the same time it does seem, paradoxically, illiberal. Even if welfare were a public good, and I have suggested that it is not, how can we know that those who desire it also desire it to be delivered in the form suggested by Friedman?

Welfare Policy and Classical Liberalism

There is no avoiding the conclusion that the provision of state welfare involves a loss in liberty, an attenuation of choice and therefore a restriction of the domain of the market. The rationale of this may be paternalist; and it usually involves the invocation of some explicit redistributive principles, such as social justice or equality. Because these values are not universally accepted within a community (indeed, their very *meaning* is by no means uncontroversial so that they have been rightly called 'essentially contested' concepts) the institutions and policies of the welfare state are subject to continual dispute. This is why the arguments for the welfare state (citizenship, rights, equality and so on) seem so often to be elegant rationalisations of a policy position accepted on other, perhaps intuitive, grounds. Indeed, when the existing policies of the welfare state are set against their justificatory principles (as in the discussion about equality) they often seem to be no more than a set of vague, *ad hoc* and self-contradictory maxims. In this sense, the contribution of classical liberalism to the analysis of the welfare state is largely negative (though no less important for that). Its major conclusion must be that there is no objective and indisputable rationale from which determinate policies can be inferred.

One important reason why this is so is the fact that welfare state principles are held in conjunction with democratic choice principles. What we have in the way of deprivation-relieving policies must in some way reflect choice — that expressed through either the market or the state. For this reason classical liberals, who of course do accept the necessity of some public decision-making, must also accept that individuals as voters will demand that public authorities play a welfare role. There is no clear-cut distinction, based on 'efficiency' grounds, between the public and private domains as is implied in the traditional books on welfare economics.

Democracy, Welfare and Liberty

However, there is clearly a role for classical liberalism in examining critically the procedures through which the subjective choice for public welfare is transmitted.[1] The repeated exposures of the 'middle-class capture' of the welfare state illustrate the necessity of this. Present majority-rule democratic procedures encourage groups to seek privileges through the welfare state, even though each individual group member may have a benevolent preference.[2] Nevertheless, it has to be conceded that a classical liberal 'constitutional' welfare theory has yet to be developed.

There is, however, one argument that, if true, would be effective, if not decisive, in rebutting the classical liberal's plea for some kind of constitutional truce between the market and the state. It is that if the market could be shown to be autonomy-reducing, and the causal agent in the production of avoidable deprivation, then this would constitute at least a *prima facie* case for intervention on grounds of moral principle. Is this so? Or can the market be absolved from this type of moral 'blame'?

The Market Versus the State Again

One of the major arguments for the market, adumbrated by Adam Smith, and even before him by Bernard Mandeville, and echoed repeatedly today, is that the exchange system driven by self-interest will accidentally maximise welfare more effectively than the deliberate prosecution of the public good. Although market incentives produce inequalities, the increased expenditure of the rich will generate higher employment that will lead to a trickle-down effect by which the conditions of the poor are gradually improved. As the saying goes: 'the luxuries of

---

[1] See Brennan, G. and Buchanan, J., *The Reason of Rules*, Cambridge: Cambridge University Press, 1986.

[2] This, in essence, is the 'economic theory of democracy'.

today are the necessities of tomorrow'. Despite its inequalities, the market raises the well-being of the worst off more effectively than welfarist egalitarianism.

This is partly an empirical argument, which is in fact confirmed in a rough and ready way by a comparison between communist and capitalist regimes. However, it should be stressed that the trickle-down effect is notoriously difficult to measure. One crucially important point is the time factor. The increased prosperity brought about by the recognised efficiency of market capitalism cannot be expected to filter through to all sections of society overnight. This observation is especially pertinent to those economic systems which undergo a change from a 'mixed' or semi-socialist form to a much more capitalist arrangement; for the necessary reallocation of the factors of production to more socially efficient uses is certain to leave pockets of temporary unemployment and deprivation. Indeed, there is a genuine case for public welfare here. But the rationale for it can hardly be derived from market 'failure', since the introduction of markets comes about because of observed deficiencies of collectivist planning. The existence of social deprivation can have many causes, including mistaken action by the state (and, indeed, personal improvidence): a point frequently overlooked.

Trickle Down?

However, Kenneth Hoover and Raymond Plant claim (albeit cautiously) that in Britain (from 1978 to 1987) the 'Thatcher years' have not produced a trickle-down effect to any great extent.[1] Although they concede that there has been a small increase in real income even for the poorest, the evidence of increased homelessness, widening inequalities in wages, increasing numbers of people relying upon welfare benefits, and stark disparities between the regions, are features that

---

[1] Hoover and Plant, *Conservative Capitalism, op. cit.*, Chapter 12.

describe a divided society in which only a minority have experienced significant advantages from the movement towards market capitalism.

I think there are two points relevant to this critique, and to other similar ones. First, it is an abiding temptation for social welfare theorists to treat measures of inequality as if they were data about absolute poverty. Just because certain groups of people do not share equally with other groups a general increase in prosperity it does not at all follow that the (admittedly) minimal 'welfare criterion' of market capitalism — that the system increases the well-being of the poorest irrespective of the positions of others — has not been satisfied. We often have to make uncomfortable, and sometimes distasteful, choices between, for example, a situation in which the worse off do better under capitalism even though the system produces a perhaps morally unsightly inequality, and one in which, although people are more or less equal, everybody is worse off than is economically feasible. Are we really prepared to sacrifice the well-being of individuals on behalf of a beguiling, but surely elusive, ideal? The *historical* evidence of market capitalism is surely that it does improve the absolute conditions of the least endowed in terms of resources and talents.

'Laws' of Distribution?

Second, it should be noted that I have somewhat generously assumed that economic equality is a feasible goal, that there is a genuine option of preferring a more egalitarian distribution even if that were to lead to a small loss in social efficiency. This might be thought to be theoretically possible in advanced industrial societies. However, not only is social and economic equality a notoriously difficult goal to formulate but in practice it has proved a chimera. It seems that if inequalities are repressed in one area of social life they will reappear in another. John Stuart Mill[1] once made a famous distinction between the 'laws' of production of an economy (which were assumed by him to be immutable) and the 'laws' of distribution (which were amenable to alteration by the human will) and it is this alleged difference that has validated most egalitarian social philosophies throughout the twentieth century. However, it is just as plausible to suppose that the 'laws' of distribution are also more or less fixed, if not quite so rigidly. As I noted earlier, inequalities have as much to do with certain features of the human condition as they have with differing social and economic systems, if not more so.

At least the inequalities of market capitalism are, to a great extent, 'functional' (in the sense used by T.H. Marshall). For without the prospect of gain it is difficult to imagine individuals being motivated to power the markets in order that the trickle-down effect can operate. It is surely not implausible to suggest that the rather slow drip of this 'effect' is a consequence of impediments to that 'entrepreneurial' drive on which efficiency and prosperity depend.

State Failure

One spectacular example is the rise in homelessness in Britain in the last ten years (in fact, it is a tendency that has been going on longer than this) which is used by Hoover and Plant as an example of the failure of trickle down.[2] Yet it is an unfortunate example, for almost all economists, individualist and collectivist, agree that the housing market has been almost wrecked by successive counter-productive interventions.[3] Rent controls and security of tenure simply reduce the supply of rented accommodation and privilege those lucky enough to be in the properties. Landlords will not let their property if they

---

[1] John Stuart Mill, *Principles of Political Economy*, first published in 1848.

[2] Hoover and Plant, *Conservative Capitalism*, op. cit., p. 265.

[3] See Martin Ricketts, *Lets into Leases*, London: Centre for Policy Studies, 1987.

cannot secure a reasonable return; they will sell it to the owner-occupied sector. Tax relief on mortgage interest encourages people to over-invest in housing, which raises the price to first-time buyers and produces large and untaxed capital gains for those early into the market. All this intervention has produced the bizarre paradox of an excess of housing units alongside growing numbers of homeless. It is the most well-documented case of state failure, yet it is repeatedly cited as market failure.

Other examples of social distress are not so easily explained but it is surely imperative to seek out their *cause* before recommending immediate social intervention.[1] If it is the case that deprivation is a consequence of mistaken government intervention, then many social problems, though clearly not all, would be soluble in precisely the opposite ways to those suggested by the social welfare school. Even the increase in numbers on social welfare can be partly explained by the attractions of this life-style compared to low-paid work. The depressing implication of Charles Murray's work is that there is no system of welfare that will not induce more people to become beneficiaries than was intended; the problem of 'moral hazard'. This phenomenon was known by the pessimistic social scientists of the nineteenth century.

Markets and Justice

Irrespective of these phenomena, which are, I believe, amenable to scientific investigation, there is still the moral question, posed most penetratingly by Raymond Plant,[2] of whether even a well-functioning market system can satisfy standards of justice. The more precise question is whether the standard classical liberal view of justice, i.e. that the concept should be confined to the impartial application of abstract rules involving

---

[1] See Barry, N.P., 'Classical Liberalism and Public Policy, *Il Politico*, 24, 1988.

[2] Raymond Plant summarised in Hoover and Plant, *Conservative Capitalism*, *op. cit.*, Chapter 10. For a critique of Plant's argument, see Green, *The New Right*, *op. cit.*, p. 128.

no more than equality before the law, the enforcement of the rules of contract, tort, and property, and the maintenance of a system of criminal law, is persuasive. It is a system of procedural rules, and an injustice is simply a breach of its provisions. Justice is not concerned with the 'outcomes' of impersonal market forces (e.g. distributions of income, wealth and distinctions of status) that may occur, since no one intended them. Furthermore, these outcomes are not foreseeable, because of the inevitable flux of market society. Although we may have a general supererogatory duty to tend to its 'victims' (and this is the classical liberal justification for a residual welfare state) it is not one that is strictly enforceable.

Against this, Plant argues that although the outcomes of a market are unintended they are, nevertheless, in some circumstances foreseeable and hence alterable. Despite the uncertainty and flux that characterise market systems, it is presumably true that the process of change will leave identifiable victims, and although there are no identifiable agents responsible for such deprivation there are 'surrogate offenders', i.e. impersonal market forces. To sit idly by and do nothing, when aid could be given at little cost, would not simply be uncharitable, it would be unjust.

Justifying a Minimal Welfare State

Now, although this argument has little force against the dogged believer in indefeasible natural rights, it is effective, to some extent, against the more overtly utilitarian defender of capitalism. The reason is that since writers in this tradition *ultimately* value capitalism because it does make everyone better off, outcomes must be important. And since it is known that some unpleasant side-effects of unrestrained market forces do occur, and could be avoided, then not to take action could be said, in a convoluted way, to be contributory to those consequences. This attribution of 'responsibility' does not depend at all on 'intentions': it is simply that the inactivity in a sense brought about the consequences. If the only things that matter morally are outcomes, and if unpleasant ones could be avoided, then it would be a breach of moral duty not to take appropriate action. Injustices then are generated as much by acts of *omission* as *commission*, and since they are injustices the state has an obligation to provide the remedies.

I think that some minimal welfare state (and not one based on mere benevolence) could be justified philosophically along these lines but I do not think it would be the vast, inefficient and inequitable system with which we are familiar. Neither would it uphold an egalitarian redistribution of income and wealth. In practice, it would be primarily, but not exclusively, addressed to the potential victims of *government* intervention. This means that in any serious transition from a welfare society to a full market society the authorities (no matter how *laissez-faire* they are) must uphold those entitlements to, say, pensions, unemployment insurance and so on, which are already in existence, however inefficient and immoral their foundations might be.

Conclusion

My comments throughout this paper have been of a sceptical kind, even negative. They have been critical of both classical liberal and 'social welfare' approaches to familiar problems rather than suggestive of new schemes. A healthy dose of pessimism, if not outright despair, may be what is required in the present debate. However, one positive conclusion is clear: that whatever welfare institutions and policies we have, and undoubtedly some will be generated by the transmission of benevolent preferences through the voting process, they should be directed towards making the market work better (*Markt-konform* was a nice word used by the theorists of the German 'social market economy' to describe this imperative). Markets maximise welfare and therefore their wide spread would increase individual satisfactions. Yet many social welfare theorists assume that markets are causal agents in the production of deprivation so that almost all their policies are in practice directed against the market. In housing, education, health care, pensions and so on, statist prescriptions, as some perceptive socialist economists have noted, produce poor results because they replace markets by politics.

Hence, the sceptic might well argue that the 'market versus state' debate is misconceived since the phrase implies that there are two social institutions which are forever in contention: that acceptable welfare requires the obliteration of one by the other rather than some accord between the two. However, a different policy implication might be that the state has the greatest moral licence to intervene, not where there is market failure, but where markets have nothing to do with the problem: I refer here to the uninsurable vicissitudes of life, such as serious mental and physical handicap. Even the argument that the market is condemnable because it produces selfish sentiments and attenuates that altruistic attitude required for the amelioration of the plight of the victims is misconceived. As I have shown, there is no evidence that the continual politicisation of our social life reduces the supply of self-interest.

Liberty and Welfare

Citizenship is not undermined by the penetration of social life by the market; nor is it enhanced by transferring to the state the individual's responsibility for the government of many aspects of his own life. To prevent the corruption of the welfare system and reduce the dependence of individuals on it, would require an array of positive duties by the individual towards the state which are inconsistent with the traditional liberal idea of citizenship. This is a crucial point that the neo-conservative, Lawrence Mead, is quite right to stress. If the preservation of the welfare state were to require such positive duties from its citizens, it might not be worth having. Certainly hard choices have to be made between liberty and welfare.

None of this essay is meant to imply that there is no role for the state in the supply of welfare, or that market institutions and voluntary activity are sufficient to generate all that is desirable in a civilised society.[1] All that is being suggested is that the typical welfare philosophies do not always cohere with the conventional policies of the welfare state, nor are they necessarily compatible with other values that are held to be essential for a liberal and democratic society.

---

[1] For an intriguing explanation of the way in which public welfare may be produced voluntarily, largely through the emergence of the moral principle of reciprocity, see Robert Sugden, *The Economics of Rights, Co-operation and Welfare*, Oxford: Blackwell, 1986.

Other Health and Welfare Unit Publications

Medicines in the Marketplace

June 1987, £5.95

DAVID G. GREEN, *Director, IEA Health Unit*

'If David Green's paper, the first in a series to be published by this unit, is anything to go by, a series of fascinating debates is due to follow ... Dr Green packs in a wealth of information to support his clearly stated argument, which makes what could be a boring subject into a really good read.'   *Nursing Standard*

'Green's criticisms have some merit.'   *British Medical Journal*

Efficiency and the NHS: A Case for Internal Markets?

February 1988, £4.50

RAY ROBINSON, *Kings Fund Institute*

'... the best critique so far of the internal market.'
The Independent, Guide to the NHS Debate

'An internal market would take the power of decision-making about treatment even further away from patients. "It would be district general managers who would make block decisions about where patients should be treated", Mr Robinson says.'   *The Times*

Acceptable Inequalities: Essays on the Pursuit of Equality in Health Care

April 1988, £4.00

RUDOLF KLEIN, *Professor of Social Policy, University of Bath*

ROBERT PINKER, *Professor of Social Work Studies, London School of Economics*

PETER COLLISON, *Professor of Social Studies, University of Newcastle upon Tyne*

A. J. CULYER, *Professor of Economics, University of York*

'An interesting and provocative book ...'   *British Medical Journal*

'... stimulating reading and will help ensure that this particular debate remains high on the health agenda.'   *Health Education Journal*

Keeping the Lid on Costs? Essays on Private Health Insurance and Cost-Containment in Britain
September 1988, £5.95

WILLIAM LAING, *Senior Partner, Laing and Buisson*

RAY FORMAN, *Managing Director, PPP*

NANCY SALDANA, *Head of Hospital Negotiations, PPP*

BRIAN BRICKNELL, *Personal Membership Director, BUPA*

'This short book sets a new standard of frankness about the problems of the private sector, not just in controlling costs but in maintaining quality of care ... This IEA health unit paper is a useful contribution.'

The Health Service Journal

American Health Care: What are the Lessons for Britain?
January 1989, £5.95. ISBN 0-255 36254-4

PROFESSOR CLARK C. HAVIGHURST, *Professor of Law, Duke University*

DR ROBERT B. HELMS, *Assistant Secretary, US Department of Health and Human Services, Washington*

CHRISTOPHER BLADEN, *Department of Health and Human Services*

PROFESSOR MARK PAULY, *Professor of Economics, University of Pennsylvania*

'A report ... from the Institute of Economic Affairs health unit, an influential think tank ... which attacks the "restrictive practices" operated by the medical establishment ...'
Sunday Times

'Restrictive practices enjoyed by doctors should be scrapped ... a report from the Institute of Economic Affairs says today.'
Daily Telegraph

Should Doctors Advertise?
March 1989, £3.00. ISBN 0-255 36255-2

DAVID G. GREEN, *Director, IEA Health Unit*

'The General Medical Council should be stripped of its power to interfere with doctors' advertising because it obstructs competition, said Dr David Green.'
British Medical Journal

'Despite claims that [professional] disciplinary codes protect the public, they are seen to serve the interests of bad and indifferent doctors by David Green.'
Health Service Journal

Competing for the Disabled

September 1989, £5.00. ISBN 0-255 36256-0

PROFESSOR C. S. B. GALASKO, *Consultant Orthopaedic Surgeon, Manchester*
PROFESSOR IAN McCOLL, *Director of Surgery, Guys Hospital*
CAROLINE LIPKIN, *IEA Health Unit*

'It would be wrong to this IEA publication as simply another broad right-wing sideswipe at state-funded health provision. It offers a level of detail and thoughtfulness which is likely to appeal beyond its normal constituency.' *Health Service Journal*

If you need a wheelchair you are advised to be rich ... Governments should not, [the authors] conclude, both finance and control the production of health care services, since the disadvantages are borne by the disabled.' *The Lancet*

Perestroika in the Universities

November 1989, £5.00. ISBN 0-255 36257-9

PROFESSOR ELIE KEDOURIE, *London School of Economics*

'The Government was yesterday accused of seeking to "nationalise" the universities by increasing central control over their activities through the new Universities Funding Council. Professor Kedourie said it was "quite mysterious" that a Conservative administration should follow a university policy "so much at variance with its proclaimed ideals".' *The Times*

Medical Care: Is it a Consumer Good?

April 1990, £3.95. ISBN 0-255 36258-7

BRENDAN DEVLIN, *Consultant Surgeon, North Tees General Hospital*
IAIN HANHAM, *Consultant Radiotherapist and Oncologist, Westminster Hospital*
JAMES LE FANU, *General Practitioner*
ROBERT LEFEVER, *General Practitioner*
BRIAN MANTELL, *Consultant in Radiotherapy and Oncology, The London Hospital*
MICHAEL FREEMAN, *Consultant Orthopaedic Surgeon, The London Hospital*

'Devlin ... points out that the quality of practice is by no means assured: doctors, he claims, do not always elicit the correct history, and they can overlook or misinterpret physical signs; 30-40% of appendices removed in Britain show no evidence of appendicitis.' *The Lancet*